ANTON CHEKHOV

A Journey to the End
of the Russian Empire

Translated by ROSAMUND BARTLETT,
ANTHONY PHILLIPS, LUBA TERPAK
and MICHAEL TERPAK

GREAT
JOURNEYS

TED SMART

PENGUIN BOOKS

Published by the Penguin Group
Penguin Books Ltd, 80 Strand, London WC2R ORL, England
Penguin Group (USA) Inc., 375 Hudson Street, New York, New York 10014, USA
Penguin Group (Canada), 90 Eglinton Avenue East, Suite 700, Toronto, Ontario, Canada M4P 2Y3
(a division of Pearson Penguin Canada Inc.)
Penguin Ireland, 25 St Stephen's Green, Dublin 2, Ireland (a division of Penguin Books Ltd)
Penguin Group (Australia), 250 Camberwell Road, Camberwell, Victoria 3124, Australia
(a division of Pearson Australia Group Pty Ltd)
Penguin Books India Pvt Ltd, 11 Community Centre, Panchsheel Park, New Delhi – 110 017, India
Penguin Group (NZ), 67 Apollo Drive, Rosedale, North Shore 0632, New Zealand
(a division of Pearson New Zealand Ltd)
Penguin Books (South Africa) (Pty) Ltd, 24 Sturdee Avenue, Rosebank, Johannesburg 2196, South Africa

Penguin Books Ltd, Registered Offices: 80 Strand, London WC2R ORL, England

www.penguin.com

Taken from *A Life in Letters* and *The Island: A Journey to Sakhalin*
This extract published in Penguin Books 2007

3

A Life in Letters translation copyright © Rosamund Bartlett and Anthony Phillips, 2004
Part two reprinted with the permission of Simon and Schuster Adult Publishing Group
from *The Island: A Journey to Sakhalin* by Anton Chekhov
Copyright © 1967 by Washington Square Press
All rights reserved

The moral right of the translators has been asserted

Inside-cover maps by Jeff Edwards

Typeset by Rowland Phototypesetting Ltd, Bury St Edmunds, Suffolk
Printed in England by Clays Ltd, St Ives plc

ISBN: 978-0-141-02550-6

This edition produced for The Book People Ltd,
Hall Wood Avenue, Haydock, St. Helens, WA11 9UL

Contents

Anton Chekhov (1860–1904) left his comfortable and successful life in Moscow in 1890 to travel to the desolate far eastern island of Sakhalin. He described his journey to Sakhalin through the Russian Empire, across Siberia, in a series of letters from which the first part of this book is taken. The Russian government used the island of Sakhalin as a place of exile for its most dangerous prisoners. Chekhov visited the penal settlements and wrote about the island and its notorious penal colony in a powerful description of exile and isolation, sympathetically depicting humanity in the midst of the greatest physical and cultural barrenness. Chekhov's *The Island: A Journey to Sakhalin* was first published in 1893; the second part of this book is extracted from this account.

Part 1: Letters from the Eastern Empire

1. To Alexey Suvorin, 20 May 1890, Tomsk

At long last greetings from Siberian Man, dear Alexey Sergeyevich! I have been missing both you and our correspondence terribly.

I shall nevertheless start from the beginning. They told me in Tyumen that there would be no steamer to Tomsk until 18 May. I had to take horses. For the first three days every joint and tendon in my body ached, but then I got used to it and had no more pain. But as a result of the lack of sleep, the constant fussing with the baggage, the bouncing up and down and the hunger, I suffered a haemorrhage that rather spoilt my mood, which was not in any case particularly sunny. The first few days were bearable, but then a cold wind started to blow, the heavens opened and the rivers overflowed into the fields and the roads, so that I kept having to swap my vehicle for a boat. The attached pages will tell you about my battles with the floods and the mud; I didn't mention in them that the heavy boots I had bought were too tight, so that I had to plough through mud and water in felt boots which rapidly turned into jelly. The road is so bad that in the last few days I've only managed to cover forty miles or so.

[. . .]

I've been as hungry as a horse all the way. I filled my belly with bread in order to stop thinking of turbot, asparagus and suchlike. I even dreamt of buckwheat kasha. I dreamt of it for hours on end.

I bought some sausage for the journey in Tyumen, if you can call it a sausage! When you bit into it, the smell was just like going into a stable at the precise moment the coachmen are removing their foot bindings; when I started chewing it, my teeth felt as if they had caught hold of a dog's tail smeared with tar. Ugh! I made two attempts to eat it and then threw it away.

[. . .]

Oh Lord, my expenses are mounting up! Thanks to the floods I had to pay all the coachmen almost twice and sometimes three times as much as usual, for they had to work hellishly hard, it was like penal servitude. My suitcase, a nice little trunk, has proved not to be very suitable for the journey: it takes up too much room, bashes me continually in the ribs as it rattles about, and, worst of all, is threatening to fall to pieces. 'Don't take trunks on a long journey' well-meaning people told me, but I only remembered this when I had got halfway. What to do? Well, I have decided to let my trunk take up residence in Tomsk, and have bought myself some piece of shit made of leather, but which has the advantage of flopping on the floor of a tarantass[1] and adopting

---

[1] An old-fashioned four-wheeled carriage pulled by three horses, which could travel at a speed of about 8 mph.

any shape you like. It cost me 16 roubles. Anyway, to continue ... It would be sheer torture to take post-chaises all the way to the Amur. I would simply be shaken to pieces with all my belongings. I was advised to buy my own carriage. So I bought one today for 130 roubles. If I don't succeed in selling it when I get to Sretensk, where the overland part of my journey ends, I shall be left without a penny and will howl. Today I dined with Kartamyshev, the editor of *The Siberian Herald*. He's a local Nozdryov,[2] a flamboyant sort of fellow ... Drank six roubles' worth.

Stop press! I have just been informed that the Assistant Chief of Police wants to see me. What can I have done?!?

False alarm. The policeman turned out to be a lover of literature and even a bit of a writer; he came to pay his respects. He's gone home to collect a play he's written; apparently he intends to entertain me with it ... He'll be back in a moment and again interrupt my writing to you ...

Write and tell me about Feodosia, about Tolstoy, the sea, the goby, the people we both know.

Greetings, Anna Ivanovna! God bless you. I often think of you.

Regards to Nastyusha and Borya. If it would give them pleasure I shall be delighted to throw myself into the jaws of a tiger and summon them to my aid, but alas! I haven't got as far as tigers yet. The only furry

---

[2] A character in Gogol's *Dead Souls*, portrayed as a drunken bully and a braggart.

animals I've seen so far in Siberia have been hundreds of hares and one mouse.

Stop press! The policeman has returned. He didn't read me his play, although he did bring it with him, but regaled me instead with a story he had written. It wasn't bad, a bit too local though. He showed me a gold ingot, and asked me if I had any vodka. I cannot recall any occasion on which a Siberian has not, on coming to see me, asked for vodka. This one told me he had got himself embroiled in a love affair with a married woman, and showed me his petition for divorce addressed to the highest authority. Thereupon he suggested a tour of Tomsk's houses of pleasure.

I've now returned from the houses of pleasure. Quite revolting. Two a.m.

What has Alexey Alexeyevich gone to Riga for? You wrote to me about this. How is his health? From now on I'll write to you punctually from every town and every station where I change horses, i.e. everywhere I have to spend the night. What a pleasure it is to have to stop for the night! Scarcely do I flop into bed but I'm asleep. Out here, when you keep going through the night without stopping, sleep becomes the most treasured prize there is; there is no greater pleasure on earth than sleep when you are tired. I now realize that in Moscow or indeed in Russia generally I have never really craved sleep. I just went to bed because it was time to do so. Not like now! Another thing I've noticed: you have no desire to drink when travelling. I haven't drunk a thing. I have smoked a lot though. I don't seem to be able to think properly; my thoughts just don't cohere. The time goes very quickly, so that you hardly notice it's moved on from ten o'clock in the morning to seven o'clock in the evening; the evening simply flows seamlessly into the morning. It's like being ill for a long time. My face is covered in fish scales because of all the wind and rain, so that when I look in the mirror I hardly recognize my former distinguished features.

I won't describe Tomsk. All Russian towns are the same. Tomsk is a dull and rather drunken sort of place; no beautiful women at all, and Asiatic lawlessness. The most notable thing about Tomsk is that governors come here to die.

I embrace you warmly. I kiss both Anna Ivanovna's hands and bow to the ground before her. It's raining. Goodbye, keep well and happy. You mustn't complain if my letters are short, slapdash or dry, because one is not always oneself while on the road and cannot write exactly as one would wish. This ink is appalling, and there always seem to be little bits of hair and other things sticking to the pen.

Your

A. Chekhov

[. . .]

2. *To Chekhov Family, 20 May 1890, Tomsk*

Dear Tungus friends! It's already Whitsuntide where you are, but here not even the willows have begun to come out and there is still snow on the banks of the Tom. I leave tomorrow for Irkutsk. I've had a rest. There was no particular point in hurrying on as the steamers across Lake Baikal don't start until 10 June, but now I'm on my way anyhow.

I am alive, in good health, and have not lost any of my money; the only problem is a slight soreness in my right eye, which is aching.

Everyone is telling me to return via America, since you apparently die of boredom sailing with the Voluntary Fleet: too much official military stuff, and you hardly ever put in to port.

Kuzovlyov, the customs officer who was exiled here from Taganrog, died two months ago in extreme poverty.

Having nothing better to do, I set down some travel impressions and sent them to *New Times*; you'll be able to read them some time after 10 June. I didn't go into anything in much detail. I was writing off the cuff – not for glory but for money, and to pay off some of the advance I received.

Tomsk is a most boring town. To judge from the drunks I have met and the supposedly intelligent people who have come to my room to pay their respects, the local inhabitants are deadly boring. At all events I find their company so disagreeable that I have given instructions that I am not receiving anyone.

I've been to the bathhouse and had some laundry done – five copecks a handkerchief! I bought some chocolate from sheer boredom.

Thanks to Ivan for the books; I can relax now. Please

send him my regards if he's not with you. I have written to Father, and would have written to Ivan except that I don't know for certain where he is living or where he has gone.

In two and a half days' time I shall be in Krasnoyarsk, and in seven and a half or eight days in Irkutsk. Irkutsk is a thousand miles from here.

I've just made some coffee and am about to drink it. It's morning, and the bells will soon start ringing for late mass.

The taiga[3] starts at Tomsk. So we'll see.

Best regards to all the Lintvaryovs and to our dear old Maryushka. I hope Mama won't worry and will pay no attention to bad dreams. Are the radishes ripe yet? There are none at all here.

Well, stay alive and healthy, and don't worry about money, there will be enough. Don't spoil the summer by skimping too much.

Your
A. Chekhov

My soul is crying out. Have mercy on me, my poor old trunk will be left behind in Tomsk and I'm buying myself a new one, soft and flat, which I can sit on, and which won't fall to bits from all the shaking around. So my poor old trunk has been condemned to end its days in exile in Siberia.

---

[3] Northern coniferous forest.

3. *To Chekhov Family, 25 May 1890, Mariinsk*

Spring has begun; the fields are turning green, the leaves are coming out, and there are cuckoos and even nightingales singing. It was wonderful early this morning, but at ten o'clock a cold wind started blowing, and it began to rain. It was very flat up to Tomsk, and after Tomsk it was forests, ravines and such like.

I sentenced my poor trunk to exile in Tomsk for its unwieldiness, and purchased instead (for 16 roubles!) a ridiculous object that now sprawls inelegantly on the floor of my carriage. You may now boast to everyone that we own a carriage. In Tomsk I bought a barouche with a collapsible hood etc. for 130 roubles, but needless to say it has no springs, as no one in Siberia acknowledges springs. There are no seats, but the floor is large enough and flat enough to let you stretch out full length. Travelling will be very comfortable now; I fear neither the wind nor the rain. The only thing I do fear is broken bones, because the road is truly terrible. I am endlessly getting on boats: twice this morning, and tonight we have to cover three miles by water. I am alive, and quite well.

Be well,
Your
Antoine

[. . .]

4. *To Alexander Chekhov, 5 June 1890, Irkutsk*

European brother!

Siberia is a big, cold country. There seems no end to the journey. There is little of novelty or interest to be seen, but I am experiencing and feeling a lot. I've battled with rivers in flood, with cold, unbelievable quagmires, hunger and lack of sleep . . . Experiences you couldn't buy in Moscow for a million roubles. You should come to Siberia! Get the courts to exile you here.

The best of the Siberian towns is Irkutsk. Tomsk is not worth a brass farthing, and none of the local districts is any better than that Krepkaya in which you were so careless as to be born. The worst of it is that in these little provincial places there is never anything to eat, and when you're on the road this becomes a matter of capital importance! You arrive in a town hungry enough to eat a mountain of food, and bang go your hopes; no sausage, no cheese, no meat, not so much as a herring, nothing but the sort of tasteless eggs and milk you find in the villages.

Generally I'm happy with my journey and glad that I came. It's hard going, but on the other hand it's a wonderful holiday. I'm enjoying my vacation.

After Irkutsk I go on to Lake Baikal, which I shall cross by steamer. Then it's 660 miles to the Amur, and from there I take a boat to the Pacific. The first thing I shall do when I get there is have a swim and eat oysters.

I arrived here yesterday and immediately made my way to the baths, then went to bed and slept. Oh, how I slept! Only now do I understand the true meaning of the word.

[. . .]

Blessings be upon you with both hands.
Your Asiatic brother A. Chekhov

5. *To Chekhov Family, 6 June 1890, Irkutsk*

Greetings, dearest Mama, Ivan, Masha and Misha and everyone. I am with you in spirit . . .

In the last long letter I wrote to you I said that the mountains round Krasnoyarsk resembled the Don ridge, but this is not really the case: looking at them from the street, I could see that they surrounded the town like high walls, and they reminded me strongly of the Caucasus. And when I left town in the early evening and crossed over the Enisei, I saw that the mountains on the far bank were really like the mountains of the Caucasus, with the same kind of smoky, dreamy quality . . . The Enisei is a wide, fast-flowing, lithe river, more beautiful than the Volga. The ferry across is wonderful, very skilfully designed in the way it goes against the current; I'll tell you more about its construction when I'm home. So the mountains and the Enisei have been the first genuinely new and original things I have encountered in Siberia. The feelings

I experienced when I saw the mountains and the Enisei paid me back a hundredfold for all the hoops I had to jump through to get here, and made me curse Levitan for being so foolish as not to come with me.

Between Krasnoyarsk and Irkutsk there is nothing but taiga. The forest is no denser than at Sokolniki, but no coachman can tell you where it ends. It seems endless; it goes on for hundreds of miles. Nobody knows who or what may be living in the taiga, but sometimes it happens in winter that people come down from the far north with their reindeer in search of bread. When you are going up a mountain and you look up and down, all you see are mountains in front of you, more mountains beyond them, and yet more mountains beyond them, and mountains on either side, all thickly covered in forest. It's actually quite frightening. That was the next new experience I had . . .

Beyond Krasnoyarsk the heat and the dust began. The heat is terrible, and I have banished my coat and hat. The dust gets into your mouth, up your nose, down your neck – ugh! To get to Irkutsk you must cross the Angara on a flat-bottomed ferry; and just then, as if on purpose, a strong wind gets up . . . I and the officers who are my travelling companions have spent the last ten days dreaming of a bath and a sleep in a proper bed, and we stand on the bank reluctantly getting used to the idea that we may have to spend the night in the village instead of in Irkutsk. The ferry simply cannot put in to shore . . . We wait an hour or two, and – oh heavens! – with a supreme effort the ferry gets to the bank and ties up alongside. Bravo, we can have our bath, supper, and sleep. How sweet it is to steam in the bath-house and then sleep!

Irkutsk is a splendid town, and very civilized. It has a theatre, a museum, municipal gardens with music playing in them, good hotels . . . No ugly fences with stupid posters and wasteland with notices saying it's forbidden to stay there. There is an inn called the 'Taganrog'. Sugar costs 24 copecks and pine nuts are six copecks a pound.

I was bitterly disappointed not to find a letter from you. If you had written anything before 6 May I would have received it in Irkutsk. I sent Suvorin a telegram but got no reply.

Now, about sources of filthy lucre. When you need some, write (or send a cable) to Alexander and ask him to go to the *New Times* bookshop and collect my royalties *for the books*. That's the first thing. The second is, read the enclosed letter carefully and post it in August. Keep the certificate of posting. I have written to Alexander.

Don't forget to look out for my winning ticket.

Did I write to Misha telling him that I shall probably come home via America? There's no need for him to rush off to Japan.

I am alive and well, and I haven't lost any of the money. I'm saving some of the coffee for Sakhalin. I'm drinking excellent tea, after which I feel pleasantly stimulated. I see a lot of Chinese. They are a good-natured people and far from stupid. At the Bank of Siberia I was given money straight away, received cordially, treated to cigarettes and invited out to the dacha. There is a wonderful patisserie, but everything is hellishly expensive. The pavements here are made of wood.

Last night the officers and I went and had a look round the town. We heard someone shouting for help about six times; it was probably somebody being strangled. We went to look, but didn't find anyone.

[. . .]

All my clothes are creased, dirty and torn. I look like a bandit!

[. . .]

6. *To Chekhov Family, 13 June 1890, Listvenichnaya* By the shores of Lake Baikal

I'm having the most frustrating time. On 11 June, that is the day before yesterday, we left Irkutsk in the evening, in the hope of making the Baikal steamer which was departing at four o'clock in the morning. When we reached the first station, they told us that there were no horses, so we could not continue our journey and had to spend the night there. The following morning we set out again and reached the landing stage at Lake Baikal about noon. On inquiring, we were told there would not be another steamer before Friday 15 June. So all we could do was sit on the shore until Friday, look at the water, and wait. All things eventually come to an end, and usually I don't mind waiting, except that on the 20th the steamer sails from Sretensk to go down the Amur, and if we miss that one we will have to wait until the 30th for the next steamer. God have mercy, when shall I ever get to Sakhalin?

We came to Lake Baikal by way of the banks of the Angara, which flows out of Baikal until it gets to the Enisei. Have a look at the map. The banks are very picturesque. Mountain after mountain, and all completely covered with forest. The weather has been marvellous, calm, sunny and warm; as I was travelling I felt extraordinarily well, so well in fact I find it hard to describe. It was probably due to the rest I had had in Irkutsk and to the fact that the banks of the Angara are just like Switzerland. Somehow new and original. We followed them until we came to the mouth of the river, then turned left, and there was the shore of Lake Baikal, which in Siberia they call a sea. Just like a mirror. You can't see the other shore, of course: it's more than fifty miles away. The shoreline is steep, high, rocky and tree-clad; to the right and to the left are promontories which you can see jutting out into the sea like those of Ayu-Dag or Tokhtabel near Feodosia. It's like the Crimea. The Listvenichnaya station is situated right by the water's edge and is astonishingly like Yalta; if the houses were white it would be completely like Yalta. Except that there are no buildings up on the hills: they are too sheer and it would be impossible to build on them.

We got ourselves billeted in a sort of little barn, not

unlike one of the Kraskov dachas. The Baikal starts right outside the windows, a couple of feet below the foundations. We're paying a rouble a day. Mountains, woods, the mirror-smooth Baikal – all spoilt by the knowledge that we must stay here until Friday. What are we going to do with ourselves? Also, we don't yet know what we're going to eat. The local population eats nothing but wild garlic. There's no meat or fish; despite their promises, they haven't provided any milk for us. They fleeced us of 16 copecks for a small loaf of white bread. I bought some buckwheat and a small piece of smoked ham and asked them to cook it up into a sort of mush; it tasted awful, but there was nothing we could do. One must eat. We spent all evening going round the village looking for someone to sell us a chicken, but to no avail . . . There's plenty of vodka though! Russians are such pigs. If you ask them why they don't eat meat and fish, they will tell you that there are problems with supplies and transport and so on, but you'll find as much vodka as you want even in the most remote villages. You would think it ought to be much easier to get hold of fish and meat than vodka, which costs more and is harder to transport . . . No, the point is that it is a lot more enjoyable to sit and drink vodka than make an effort to catch fish in Lake Baikal or rear cattle.

At midnight a little steamer docked; we went to have a look at it and also to find out if there might be something to eat. We were told we could have lunch the following day, but that it was night-time now, the stove in the galley was not lit, and so on. We gave thanks for 'tomorrow' – at least there was some hope! But alas! Just then the captain came in and announced that the ship would be leaving at four in the morning for Kultuk. Great! We drank a bottle of sour beer (35 copecks) in the cafeteria, which was too small even to turn round in, and saw what looked like amber beads sitting on a plate: this was omul caviar. We went back to our quarters to sleep. The very idea of sleep has become repellent to me. Each day you have to lay your coat out on the floor wool-side up, then put your rolled-up greatcoat and a pillow at the top, and you sleep on these lumpy hillocks in your trousers and waistcoat . . . Civilization, where art thou?

Today it's raining, and Baikal is shrouded in mist. 'Most diverting' as Semashko would say. It's boring. I really should settle down to some writing, but it's hard to work when the weather is bad. The prospect before me is rather thankless; it would be all right if I were on my own, but I have these officers and an army doctor with me, and they love talking and arguing. They don't understand much, but they talk about everything. One of the lieutenants is also a bit of a Khlestakov show-off. You really need to be alone when you are travelling. It's much more interesting to sit in a coach or in your room with your own thoughts than it is to be with people. In addition to the army people a boy called Innokenty Alexeyevich is travelling with us; he's a pupil at the Irkutsk Technical School; he resembles that Neapolitan who spoke with a lisp, but nicer and more intelligent. We are taking him as far as Chita.

You must congratulate me: I managed to sell my

carriage in Irkutsk. I won't tell you how much I got for it, otherwise Mamasha will fall over in a dead faint and won't be able to sleep for five nights.

[...]

The fog has lifted. I can see clouds on the mountains. Ah, devil take it! You'd think you really were in the Caucasus . . .
Au revoir,
Your Homo Sachaliensis
A. Chekhov

7. *To Chekhov Family, 20 June 1890, Shilka, on board the steamer* Ermak

Greetings, dear household members! At last I can take off my filthy, heavy boots, my worn-out trousers, my blue shirt shiny with dust and sweat, I can wash and dress myself again like a normal human being. No more sitting in a tarantass; I am ensconced in a first-class cabin on board the Amur steamer *Ermak*. This change in my fortunes took place about ten days ago, and in the following way. I wrote to you from Listven-ichnaya to tell you about missing the Baikal steamer, which meant I would have to cross the lake not on Tuesday but on Friday, and therefore not get to the Amur steamer until 30 June. But fate can play unexpected tricks. On Thursday morning I was walking along the shore of Lake Baikal and spied smoke coming from the funnel of one of the two little steamers there. Upon my asking where she was bound for, I was told she was going 'over the sea' to Klyuyevo, having been engaged by some merchant or other to take his wagon train across to the other side of the lake. Well, we also needed to go 'over the sea', and the place we needed to get to was Boyarskaya. How far was Boyarskaya from Klyuyevo? Sixteen miles, they said. I rushed off to find my travelling companions and suggested to them that we take a chance on going to Klyuyevo instead. I say 'chance', because we risked not finding any horses when we arrived at Klyuyevo, which consists of nothing but a landing-stage and a few huts, and then we would have to sit around there and miss the Friday steamer. This would have been a worse fate than the death of Igor, since that would mean having to wait until the following Tuesday. My companions nevertheless agreed to risk it, so we collected our belongings and gaily stepped on board, heading straight for the cafeteria: anything for some soup! My kingdom for a plate of soup! The cafeteria was absolutely disgusting, and built like the smallest WC you can imagine. But the cook, a former serf from Voronezh called Grigory Ivanych, proved to be a master of his craft and fed us magnificently. The weather was calm and sunny, the turquoise waters of Lake Baikal clearer than the Black Sea. People say that in the deepest places you can see down almost as far as a mile, and indeed I myself saw rocks and mountains drowning in the turquoise water that sent shivers down my spine. The trip across Baikal was wondrous, utterly unforgettable. The only bad thing was that we were in third class, the deck being fully taken up by the merchant's wagon horses, and they were stamping about during the whole voyage like raving lunatics. These horses added a certain flavour to my voyage: I felt as if I was on some sort of pirate ship. At Klyuyevo the watchman agreed to take our luggage to the station; he set off in his cart and we followed behind on foot beside the lake through the most magnificent and picturesque scenery. It's beastly of Levitan not to have come with me! The track led through the forest: woods to the right up the mountainside, woods to the left dropping down to the lake. What ravines, what crags! The colours round Baikal are warm and gentle. The weather was very warm, by the way. After a five-mile walk we came to Myskansk station, where a passing official from Kyakhta gave us excellent tea and where we managed to get horses so that we could travel on to Boyarskaya. All this meant that we left on Thursday instead of Friday, and, better still, we got away a whole twenty-four hours ahead of the mail, which usually grabs all the horses from the station. We pressed on neck and crop, nourished by the faint hope that we might reach Sretensk by the 20th. I'll wait until I see you to tell you about my journey along the banks of the Selenga and then across Trans-Baikal, except to say that the Selenga is utterly beautiful, and in Trans-Baikal I found everything I have ever wanted: the Caucasus, the Psyol valley, the area round Zvenigorod, and the Don. In the afternoon you can be galloping through the Caucasus, by nightfall you are in the Don steppe, and next morning you wake from a doze and find yourself in Poltava – and it's like that for all six hundred miles. Verkhneudinsk is a nice little town, Chita not so nice, a bit like Sumy. Needless to say, there was no time even to think of eating or sleeping; we rattled on, changing horses at stations and worrying about whether or not there would be any horses at the next one, or whether we would have to wait there for five or six hours. We covered 130 miles a day, and that's the most you can do in summer. We were completely dazed. During the day the heat was terrible too, and then it got very cold at night, so that I had to put on my leather jacket over my cotton one; one night I even had my coat on. Well, on we went and on we went, and this morning we arrived at Sretensk, exactly one hour before the steamer sailed, having tipped the coachmen at the two last stations a rouble apiece.

And so has ended my mounted journey across the wide land. It has taken me two months (I left on 21 April), and if you don't count the time spent travelling by rail and ship, the three days I was in Ekaterinburg and the week at Tomsk, a day in Krasnoyarsk and a week in Irkutsk, two days at Baikal and the days spent waiting for floods to subside so that boats could sail, you get an idea of the rapidity of my progress. I have had as good a journey as any traveller could wish for. I have not had a day's illness, and of the mass of belongings I brought with me have lost only a penknife, the strap from my trunk and a little tub of carbolic ointment. I still have all my money. Not many can travel like that for thousands of miles.

I got so used to travelling by road that now I feel

somehow ill at ease, scarcely able to believe that I am no longer in a tarantass and am not hearing the jingling of the harness bells. It is a strange feeling to be able to stretch out my legs fully when I lie down to sleep, and for my face not to be in the dust. But the strangest thing of all is that the bottle of cognac Kuvshinnikov presented me with did not get broken and has not lost a drop. I promised him that I would uncork it on the shores of the Pacific.

We are travelling down the Shilka, which joins the Argunya at Pokrovskaya station and thence flows into the Amur. It is no wider than the Psyol, perhaps not even as wide. The banks are rocky, all cliffs and forests, and full of game. We tack from side to side in order to avoid running aground or bumping the stern against the banks – the steamers and barges are always bashing alongside one another. It's very stuffy. We have just stopped at Ust-Kara, where we disembarked five or six convicts; there are mines and a hard-labour prison there.

Yesterday I was in Nerchinsk, not exactly a brilliant little place, but one could live there, I suppose.

And how are you living, ladies and gentlemen? I am completely in the dark about how things are with you. Perhaps you could club together and find a 10-copeck piece to send me a wire.

The boat is going to tie up at Gorbitsa for the night, where I shall post this letter. The nights can be misty hereabouts and it is not safe to navigate.

I am going first class, because my travelling companions are in second class and I am keen to get away from them. We were all on the road together (three in a tarantass), slept together, and have all got fed up with each other, especially I with them.

[. . .]

My handwriting is dreadfully shaky because the boat shudders all the time. It's hard to write.

A little interlude. I went down to see my lieutenants and drink tea with them. They both slept well and are in a good mood . . . One of them, Lieutenant Schmidt (not a pleasant-sounding name to my ears), from an infantry regiment, is a tall, well-fed, loud-mouthed Courlander[4] and a real Khlestakov show-off. He sings bits from all the operas but with as much ear for music as a smoked herring. He is an unhappy, rather ill-bred fellow who has squandered his entire travel allowance, knows Mickiewicz[5] by heart, is candid to a fault and can talk the hind legs off a donkey. Like Ivanenko he loves to talk about his uncles and aunts. The other officer, Meller, is a quiet, modest cartographer and a highly intelligent fellow. If it weren't for Schmidt, one could happily go a million miles with him, but when Schmidt is around shoving his oar into every conversation, I get bored with him too. Anyhow, what do you care about these lieutenants? They are not very interesting.

[4] Courland, an historic region and former duchy in Latvia, situated between the Baltic Sea and the Western Dvina River.
[5] Adam Mickiewicz (1798–1855), the Polish national poet.

Look after your health. We seem to be approaching Gorbitsa.

Hearty greetings to the Lintvaryovs. I shall write separately to Papasha. I sent a postcard to Alyosha from Irkutsk. Farewell! I wonder when this letter will get to you? Probably it will be at least forty days from now.

I embrace and bless you all. I'm missing you.

Your

A. Chekhov

[. . .]

8. To Chekhov Family, 23–26 June 1890, en route from Pokrovskaya to Blagoveshchensk

I've already written to tell you how we ran aground. At Ust-Strelka, where the Shilka flows into the Argunya (look at the map), the ship, which draws two and a half feet of water, struck a rock which holed her in a few places, and as the hold began to take in water we settled on the bottom. They set to pumping out the water and patching the holes; one of the sailors stripped naked and crawled into the hold up to his neck in water, and felt about for the holes with his heels. Each hole was then covered from the inside with heavy sailcloth smeared with caulk, after which they placed a board over it and inserted a bracing strut on top of the board which reached up to the roof of the hold – and that was the hole repaired. They went on pumping

from five o'clock in the evening until nightfall, but the
water level did not go down; they had to stop work
until the following morning. The next morning they
discovered some more holes, so they carried on pumping and patching. The sailors pumped while we, the
passengers, strolled about the decks, gossiped, ate and
drank and slept; the captain and the first mate were
taking their cue from the passengers and were obviously
not in any hurry. To our right was the Chinese shore,
to our left the village of Pokrovskaya with its Amur
Cossacks. You could either be in Russia or you could
cross over to China – up to you, nothing to stop you
either way. During the day the heat was unbearable,
and I had to put on a silk shirt.

Lunch is served at twelve noon and supper at seven
o'clock in the evening.

By a piece of bad luck, the steamer coming in the
opposite direction, the *Herald*, with a mass of people
on board, could not get through either and both ships
have ended up stuck fast. There was a military band
on board the *Herald*, and the result was an excellent
party; all day yesterday we had music on deck which
entertained the captain and the sailors and no doubt
delayed the repairs to the ship. The female passengers
– particularly the college girls – were having a ball:
music, officers, sailors . . . ah! Yesterday evening we
went into the village, where we listened to more of the
same music, which the Cossacks had paid for. Today
the repairs are continuing. The captain is promising
that we shall be off again after dinner, but his promises
are made so languidly, his eyes wandering somewhere

off to the side, that he's obviously lying. We're not in any rush. When I asked one of the passengers when we were likely to be on our way at last, he asked: 'Aren't you enjoying being here?' And he's right, of course. Why shouldn't we stay here, so long as it's not boring?

The captain, the mate and the agent are as pleasant as can be. The Chinese down in third class are good-natured, amusing people. Yesterday one of them was sitting on the deck singing something very sad in a treble voice, and while doing so his profile was more amusing than any cartoon drawing. Everyone was watching him and laughing, but he paid not the slightest attention. Then he stopped singing treble and switched to tenor – good God, what a voice! It was like a sheep bleating or a calf mooing. The Chinese remind me of gentle, tame animals. Their pigtails are long and black, like Natalia Mikhailovna's. Mention of tame animals reminds me: there is a tame fox cub living in the bathroom, which sits and watches you while you wash. If it hasn't seen anybody for a time, it starts to whimper.

We have some very strange conversations! The only topics of conversation round here are gold, the gold fields, the Voluntary Fleet, and Japan. Every peasant in Pokrovskaya, even the priest, is out prospecting for gold. So are the exiles, who can get rich here as quickly as they can get poor. There are some nouveaux riches who won't drink anything but champagne, and who will only go to the tavern if someone puts down a red carpet for them stretching right from their hut to the door of the inn.

When autumn comes, would you please send my winter coat to the *New Times* bookshop in Odessa, first asking Suvorin's permission, which you must do for form's sake. I shan't need galoshes. Also send any letters for me and a note of your address. If you should have any spare money, you could also send 100 roubles to the same address marked for transfer to me, in case I should need them. You will need to mark them to be transferred to me, otherwise I shall have to hang about getting them from the post office. If you don't have any spare, it doesn't matter. When you get to Moscow, suggest to Father that he take some potassium bromide, because he gets dizzy spells in the autumn; if this happens you must apply a leech behind his ear. Anything else? Yes, ask Ivan to buy from Ilyin (the shop in Petrovsky Lane) a map of the Trans-Baikal area printed on cloth, and send it in a printed-matter wrapper to this address: Innokenty Alexeyevich Nikitin, pupil at the Technical School. Please keep all newspapers and letters for me.

The Amur is an extraordinarily interesting and unusual region. It seethes with life in a way that you can have no conception of in Europe. It (life here, that is) reminds me of stories I've heard about life in America. The banks of the river are so wild, so unusual and so luxuriant one wants to stay here for ever. As I write these lines it is now 25 June. The steamer vibrates so much it's hard to write. We are on our way once more. I've already travelled over six hundred miles down the Amur, and have seen a million magnificent landscapes; my head is spinning with excitement and delight. I saw one cliff that would cause Kundasova to expire in ecstasy, were she to take it into her head to oxidize herself at the foot of it, and if Sofia Petrovna Kuvsh[innikova] and I were to arrange a picnic at the top of it, we could say to one another: 'You can die now, Denis, you will never write anything better.' The landscape is amazing. And it's so hot! It's warm even at night. The mornings are misty, but still warm.

I stare at the banks through binoculars and see masses of ducks, geese, divers, herons and all manner of long-billed creatures. It would be a glorious place to rent a dacha!

Yesterday we passed a little place called Reinovo, where a man in the gold business asked me to visit his sick wife. When I left his house, he pressed a wad of banknotes into my hand. I felt guilty and tried to refuse the money, handing it back and saying that I was a rich man myself; the discussion went on for some time with each of us attempting to persuade the other, but in the end I still found I had 15 roubles left in my hand. Yesterday a gold dealer with a face just like Petya Polevayev's came to lunch in my cabin; he drank champagne throughout the meal instead of water and treated us to it as well.

The villages here are like those on the Don; the buildings are a little different, but not much. The locals don't observe Lent, and they eat meat even during Passion Week; the young women smoke cigarettes and the old ones pipes – that is the custom here. It's odd to see peasant women smoking cigarettes. What liberalism! Ah, what liberalism!

The air on board gets red hot from all the talking. Out here nobody worries about saying what he thinks. There's no one to arrest you and nowhere to exile people to, so you can be as liberal as you please. The people grow ever more independent, self-sufficient and understanding. If a conflict should arise in Ust-Kara, where there are convicts working (among them many political prisoners who aren't subject to a hard-labour regime), it would spread unrest right through the whole Amur region. There's no culture of denouncing people here. A political prisoner on the run can take a steamer all the way to the ocean without fearing that the captain will turn him in. In part this can be explained by a complete indifference to what goes on in Russia. Everybody would say: 'What has that to do with me?'

I forgot to write and tell you that the coachmen in Trans-Baikal are not Russian but Buryat.[6] They are a funny lot. Their horses are viperish; they loathe being put into harness and are crazier than horses pulling fire-engines. To harness the trace horse you first have to hobble its legs; the moment the hobble is removed, the troika takes off like a bullet, enough to take your breath away. If the horse isn't hobbled it will kick over the traces and gouge chunks out of the shafts with its hooves, tear the harness to shreds and generally give an impression of a young devil caught by his horns.

We are getting near Blagoveshchensk now. Be well and happy, and don't get too used to my not being

[6] Mongolian people whose lands were located north of the Russian –Mongolian border, near Lake Baikal.

with you. But perhaps you already have? A deep bow and an affectionate kiss to you all.

Antoine

My health is excellent.

9. *To Alexey Suvorin, 27 June 1890, Blagoveshchensk*

Greetings, dearest friend! The Amur is a very fine river indeed; I have got from it more than I could have expected, and for some time I have been wanting to share my delight with you, but for seven days the wretched boat has been juddering so much that it has prevented me from writing. Not only that, but it is quite beyond my powers to describe the beauties of the banks of the Amur; I can but throw up my hands and confess my inadequacy. Well, how to describe them? Imagine the Suram Pass in the Caucasus moulded into the form of a river bank, and that gives you some idea of the Amur. Crags, cliffs, forests, thousands of ducks, herons and all kinds of fowl with viciously long bills, and wilderness all around. To our left the Russian shore, to our right the Chinese. If I want I can look into Russia, or into China, just as I like. China is as wild and deserted as Russia: you sometimes see villages and guard huts, but not very often. My brains have addled and turned to powder, and no wonder, Your Excellency! I've sailed more than six hundred miles down the Amur, and before that there was Baikal and Trans-Baikal ... I have truly seen such riches and experienced such rapture that death holds no more terrors for me. The people living along the Amur are most unusual, and they lead interesting lives, not at all like ours. All they talk about is gold. Gold, gold – nothing else. I feel foolish and disinclined to write, so I'm writing very briefly and like a pig; I sent you four printer's sheets today about the Enisei and the taiga, and I'll send you something later about Baikal, Trans-Baikal and the Amur. Don't throw anything away; I'll collect it all up and use it for notes to tell you in person what I seem to be unable to put on paper. I have changed ships and am now on the *Muravyov*; I'm told it is a much smoother vessel, so perhaps I shall be able to write while I'm on board.

I'm in love with the Amur and would be happy to stay here for a couple of years. It is beautiful, with vast open spaces and freedom, and it's warm. Switzerland and France have never known such freedom: the poorest exile breathes more freely on the Amur than the highest general in Russia. If you were to live here you would write a lot of splendid things that would give the public a great deal of pleasure, but I am not up to it.

Beyond Irkutsk one starts to encounter the Chinese, and by the time you get here they are more numerous than flies. They are a very good-natured people. If Nastya and Borya could get to know some Chinese, they would leave their donkeys in peace and transfer their affections to the Chinese. They are nice animals and quite tame.

The Japanese start at Blagoveshchensk, or rather

Japanese women, diminutive brunettes with big, weird hair-dos. They have beautiful figures and are, as I saw for myself, rather short in the haunch. They dress beautifully. The 'ts' sound predominates in their language. When, to satisfy your curiosity, you have intercourse with a Japanese woman, you begin to understand Skalkovsky, who is said to have had his photograph taken with a Japanese whore. The Japanese girl's room was very neat and tidy, sentimental in an Asiatic kind of way, and filled with little knick-knacks – no washbasins or objects made out of rubber or portraits of generals. There was a wide bed with a single small pillow. The pillow is for you; the Japanese girl puts a wooden support under her head in order not to spoil her coiffure. The back of her head rests on the concave part. A Japanese girl has her own concept of modesty. She keeps the light on, and if you ask her what is the Japanese word for such and such a thing she answers directly, and because she doesn't know much Russian points with her fingers or even picks it up, also she doesn't show off or affect airs and graces as Russian women do. She laughs all the time and utters a constant stream of 'ts' sounds. She has an incredible mastery of her art, so that rather than just using her body you feel as though you are taking part in an exhibition of high-level riding skill. When you climax, the Japanese girl picks a piece of cotton cloth from out of her sleeve with her teeth, catches hold of your 'old man' (remember Maria Krestovskaya?) and somewhat unexpectedly wipes you down, while the cloth tickles your tummy. And all this is done with artful coquetry, accompanied by laughing and the sing-song sound of the 'ts' . . .

When I invited a Chinaman into the cafeteria to stand him a glass of vodka, he held the glass out to me, to the barman and to the waiters before drinking it, and said 'velly nice, eat!'. That is Chinese formality. He did not drink it down in one go, as we do, but in sips, nibbling something after each sip. He then thanked me by giving me some Chinese coins. Astonishingly polite people! They don't spend much money on clothes, but they dress very beautifully, and they are discriminating in what they eat, which they do with a sense of ceremony.

There is no doubt that the Chinese are going to take the Amur[7] from us. Or rather, they will not take it themselves; others will take it and give it to them, the English, for example, who control China and are building strongholds everywhere. The people who live along the Amur are a very sardonic lot; they find it highly amusing that Russia is so exercised about Bulgaria, which isn't worth a brass farthing, and pays no attention whatever to the Amur. It is an improvident and foolish attitude to take. However, the politics must wait until we meet.

You sent me a telegram saying that I should make my return journey via America. I was indeed thinking of doing just that, but people are warning me against it because of the cost. There are other places besides

[7] The Amur runs along the Russo-Chinese border and its ownership was a constant bone of contention.

New York where you can transfer money to me; you can do so in Vladivostok, through the Bank of Siberia in Irkutsk – they welcomed me warmly when I was there. I still have some funds left, although I am spending them like water. I lost more than 160 roubles on the sale of my carriage, and my travelling companions, the lieutenants, have taken more than 100 roubles off me. But, in fact, I don't think I shall need any money transferred. If the need arises I'll let you know in good time.

I am feeling extremely well. Judge for yourself – after all, I've been living out in the open day and night for more than two months now. And all that physical exercise!

I'm rushing to get this letter finished, as the *Ermak* is due to sail back in an hour's time taking the mail with it. It will be some time in August before you receive this letter.

I kiss Anna Ivanovna's hand and pray to heaven for her good health and happiness. Has Ivan Pavlovich Kazansky been to see you, the young student with the neatly pressed trousers who makes you feel depressed?

Along the way I've done a bit of doctoring. In Reinovo, a little place on the Amur inhabited exclusively by gold dealers, one of them asked me to see his pregnant wife. As I was leaving his house he pressed a wad of banknotes into my hand; I felt guilty and tried to give them back, assuring him that I was a very wealthy man and didn't need the money. It ended by my giving the packet back to him, but somehow there were still 15 roubles left in my hand. Yesterday I treated a small boy and refused the six roubles his mother thrust into my hand. I'm sorry now I didn't take them.

Be well and happy. Forgive me for writing so disgracefully and with so little detail. Have you written to me in Sakhalin?

I have been swimming in the Amur. Bathing in the Amur, talking and dining with gold smugglers – is that not an interesting life?

I must run to the *Ermak*. Farewell!

Thank you for the news about my family.

Your

A. Chekhov

10. *To Chekhov Family, 29 June 1890, near Khabarovka, on board the* Muravyov

There are meteors flying all round my cabin – fireflies, just like electric sparks. Wild goats were swimming across the Amur this afternoon. The flies here are enormous. I am sharing my cabin with a Chinaman, Son-Liu-li, who chatters incessantly about how in China they cut your head off for the merest trifle. He was smoking opium yesterday, which made him rave all night and stopped me getting any sleep. On the 27th I spent some time walking round the Chinese town of Aigun. Little by little I am entering into a fantastic world. The steamer shakes so much I can hardly write. Yesterday evening I sent Papasha a congratulatory telegram. Did it arrive all right?

The Chinaman has now launched into a song inscribed on his fan. I hope you are all well.
Your
Antoine
Regards to the Lintvaryovs.

[. . .]

11. To Alexey Suvorin, 11 September 1890, Tatar Strait, on board the Baikal

Greetings! I'm sailing south through the Tatar Strait which separates North from South Sakhalin. I have no idea when this letter will reach you. I am in good health, although from all sides I see the green eyes of cholera staring at me, waiting to ensnare me. Cholera is everywhere – in Vladivostok, Japan, Shanghai, Chifu, Suez, even on the moon it seems – quarantine and fear are everywhere. They are expecting that cholera will strike in Sakhalin, so ships are being held in quarantine; in short, things are in a bad way. Some Europeans have died in Vladivostok, among them the wife of a general.

I stayed on North Sakhalin for exactly two months, and the local administration welcomed me there with exceptional cordiality, even though Galkin had written not a word about me. Neither Galkin, nor Baroness Muskrat nor the other geniuses I was stupid enough to turn to for help, lifted a finger to help me: I had to do everything entirely on my own account.

Kononovich, the general in charge of Sakhalin, is an intelligent and decent person. We got on well together right away, and everything turned out fine. I shall bring some papers back with me which will show you that the context in which I was working was as good as it could be. I saw *everything*, so the question now is not *what* I saw, but *how* I saw it.

I don't know exactly what will come from this, but I have achieved a good deal, enough for three dissertations. I rose every morning at five o'clock, went to bed late, and laboured all day under great pressure at the thought of how much I had still to accomplish. But now that my own experience of hard labour is over, it's hard to avoid the suspicion that in seeing all the trees I missed the wood.

By the way, I patiently carried out a census of the entire population of Sakhalin. I went to all the settlements, visited every hut and talked with everyone. I used a card system to take notes, and now have records of about ten thousand convicts and settlers. In other words, there are no convicts or settlers on Sakhalin with whom I did not meet and talk. I was especially glad to be able to make records of the children, and hope that this information will prove to be of value for the future.

I dined with Landsberg[8] and sat in the kitchen of the former Baroness Heimbruck[9]. . . I visited all the

---

[8] Karl Landsberg, a guards officer exiled to Sakhalin.
[9] Baroness Olga Gembruk (Heimbruck), a convicted criminal who was exiled to Sakhalin.

celebrities. I was present at a flogging, after which I had nightmares for three or four nights about the executioner and the dreadful flogging-bench. I talked to convicts who were chained to their wheelbarrows. One day I was drinking tea in a mine, when Borodavkin, the former St Petersburg merchant who is serving a sentence here for arson, took a teaspoon out of his pocket and presented it to me. All in all it was a huge strain on my nerves and I vowed never again to come to Sakhalin.

I would like to write to you more fully, but a lady in the cabin is screaming with laughter and jabbering without ceasing, and I don't have the strength to write any more. She has been guffawing and chattering without a moment's peace since yesterday evening.

This letter will come to you via America, but I don't think I shall go that way. Everyone agrees that the route through America costs more and is more boring.

Tomorrow I shall catch a distant glimpse of the island of Matsmai, off Japan. It is now getting on for midnight, darkness is on the face of the waters and the wind is blowing. It's a mystery to me how the ship can keep going and stay on its bearings in such pitch-black conditions, not to mention in such wild and uncharted waters as the Tatar Strait.

When I remember that I am over six thousand miles away from the world I know, I feel overwhelmed with lethargy, as though it will be a hundred years before I return home.

My most profound respects and heartiest greetings

to Anna Ivanovna and all your family. May God grant you happiness and all your desires.

Your

A. Chekhov

I'm depressed.

12. To Evgenia Chekhova, 6 October 1890, South Sakhalin Island

Greetings, dear Mama! I'm writing this letter to you on what is almost the eve of my departure from here back to Russia. We wait every day for the Voluntary Fleet steamship, hoping that it will be here at the latest by 10 October. I'm sending this letter to Japan, from where it will come on to you via Shanghai, or possibly America. At present I am billeted at the Korsakovsk station, where there is no post or telegraph office, and where ships only put in once a fortnight at most. One boat did come in yesterday, bringing me a pile of letters and telegrams from the north. From them I learnt that Masha enjoyed being in the Crimea; I thought she would prefer the Caucasus. I learnt that Ivan has hopelessly failed to master the art of cooking the schoolmasterly kasha, mixing up the grains with the oats. Where is he at the moment? In Vladimir? I learnt that Mikhailo, thanks be to God, had nowhere to live all summer and so stayed at home, that you went to the Holy Mountains, and that Luka was boring and rainy. It's strange! Where you were it was rainy and cold, while from the moment I arrived in Sakhalin until today it has been warm and bright; sometimes there's a light frost in the mornings and one of the mountains has snow on the top, but the earth is still green, the leaves have not fallen and nature all around is smiling, just like May at the dacha. That's Sakhalin for you! I also found out from letters that the summer at Babkino was marvellous, that Suvorin is pleased with his house, that Nemirovich-Danchenko is not happy, that Ezhov's wife has died, poor fellow, and finally that Ivanenko and Jamais are writing to each other and that Kundasova has gone off somewhere, nobody knows where. I shall personally put Ivanenko to death, and I suppose that Kundasova is, as before, wandering the streets waving her arms about and calling everybody scum, and therefore I am not rushing to grieve for her.

At midnight yesterday I heard a ship's siren. Everyone jumped out of bed: hooray, our ship must have come in! We all got dressed, took lanterns and went down to the jetty, where indeed we saw in the distance the lights of a ship. Everyone thought it must be the *Petersburg*, the ship on which I will be sailing to Russia. I was thrilled. We climbed on board a dinghy and rowed out; we rowed, and rowed, and at last the dark bulk of the ship loomed out of the mist before us. One of us croaked out: 'Ahoy there! What ship are you?' The answer came back: *Baikal*! Oof, curses, what a disappointment! I'm homesick, and fed up with Sakhalin. After all, for three months I've seen no one besides convicts or people who have no topic of conversation other than hard labour, floggings and prisoners.

A wretched existence. I am longing to get to Japan, and then on to India.

I am very well, if you don't count a twitch in my eye which seems to be bothering me often just now, and which always seems to give me a bad headache. My eye was twitching yesterday and today, so I am writing this letter to the accompaniment of an aching head and a heaviness throughout my body. My haemorrhoids also remind me of their existence.

The Japanese Consul Kuze-San lives at Korsakovsk with his two secretaries, whom I have got to know well. They live in the European style. The local administrative establishment made an official visit today with all due pomp and circumstance, to present them with medals they had been awarded; I went along with my headache, and had to drink champagne.

While staying here in the south I went three times from the Korsakovsk station to visit Naibuchi, a place lashed by real ocean waves. Look at the map and you will find poor, benighted Naibuchi on the eastern shore of the southern island. These waves destroyed a boat with six American whalers on board; their ship was wrecked off the coast of Sakhalin and they are now living at the station, stolidly tramping the streets. They are also waiting for the *Petersburg* and will sail with me.

I sent you a letter at the beginning of September via San Francisco? Did you get it?

Greetings to Papasha, to my brothers, to Masha, to my Aunt and to Alyokha, to Maryushka, Ivanenko and all my friends. I'm not bringing any furs; there weren't any on Sakhalin. I wish you good health, and may heaven preserve you all.

Your

Anton

I'll be bringing presents for everyone. The cholera has abated in Vladivostok and Japan.

13. *To Mikhail Chekhov, 16 October 1890,* *Vladivostok*

Will be in Moscow on 10 December. Going via Singapore.

[. . .]

Part 2: Sakhalin Island

i. Across the Tatar Strait

Sakhalin lies in the Okhotsk Sea, protecting almost a thousand versts of eastern Siberian shoreline as well as the entrance into the mouth of the Amur from the ocean. It is long in form, running from north to south; its shape in the opinion of one author suggests a sturgeon. Its geographic location is from 45° 54' to 54° 53' latitude and from 141° 40' to 144° 53' longitude. The northern section of Sakhalin, which is crossed by a belt of permafrost, can be compared with Ryazan *guberniya*, the southern section with the Crimea. The island is 900 versts long, its widest portion measuring 125 versts and its narrowest 25 versts. It is twice as large as Greece and one and a half times the size of Denmark.

The former division of Sakhalin into northern, central and southern districts was impracticable, and it is now divided only into northern and southern. The upper third of the island precludes colonization due to its climatic and soil conditions. The central section is called Northern Sakhalin and the lower, Southern Sakhalin. There are no rigid boundaries between them. At the present time convicts inhabit the northern section along the Duyka and Tym Rivers; the Duyka falls into the Tatar Strait and the Tym into the Okhotsk

Sea; both rivers meet at their source according to the map. Convicts also live along the western bank in a small area above and below the Duyka estuary. Administratively, Northern Sakhalin is composed of two districts: Alexandrovsk and Tymovsk.

After spending the night at De Kastri, we sailed at noon on the next day, July 10, across the Tatar Strait to the mouth of the Duyka, where the Alexandrovsk command post is situated. The weather again was calm and bright, a rare phenomenon here. On the completely becalmed sea whales swam past in pairs, shooting fountains into the air. This lovely and unusual spectacle amused us the entire trip. But I must admit my spirits were depressed and the closer I got to Sakhalin the more uncomfortable I became. The officer in charge of the soldiers, learning of my mission in Sakhalin, was greatly amazed and began to argue that I had absolutely no right to visit the penal settlement and the colony since I was not a government official. Naturally I knew he was wrong. Nevertheless, I was greatly troubled by his words and feared that I would probably encounter the same point of view on Sakhalin.

When we cast anchor at nine o'clock, huge fires were burning at five different places on the Sakhalin taiga. I could not see the wharf and buildings through the darkness and the smoke drifting across the sea, and could barely distinguish dim lights at the post, two of which were red. The horrifying scene, compounded of darkness, the silhouettes of mountains, smoke, flames and fiery sparks, was fantastic. On my left monstrous fires were burning, above them the mountains, and beyond the mountains a red glow rose to the sky from remote conflagrations. It seemed that all of Sakhalin was on fire.

To the right, Cape Zhonkiyer reached out to sea, a long, heavy shoulder similar to the Crimean Ayu-Dag. A lighthouse shone brightly on the summit, while below in the water between us and the shore rose the three sharp reefs – 'The Three Brothers.' And all were covered with smoke, as in hell.

A cutter with a barge in tow approached the ship. Convicts were being brought to unload the freight. We could hear Tatar being spoken, and curses in Russian.

'Don't let them come on board,' someone shouted. 'Don't let them! At night they will steal everything on the boat.'

'Here in Alexandrovsk it is not so bad,' said the engineer, as he saw how depressed I was while gazing to shore. 'Wait until you see Dué! The cliffs are completely vertical, with dark canyons and layers of coal; fog everywhere! Sometimes we carried two to three hundred prisoners on the *Baikal* to Dué and many burst into tears when they saw the shore!'

'We are the prisoners, not the convicts,' said the captain. 'It is calm here now, but you should see it in the fall: wind, snow, storms, cold, the waves dash over the side of the ship – and that's the end of you!'

I spent the night on board. At five o'clock in the morning I was noisily awakened with, 'Hurry, hurry! The cutter is making its last trip to shore! We are leaving at once!' A moment later I was sitting in the cutter. Next to me was a young official with an angry, sleepy face. The cutter sounded its whistle and we left for the shore towing two barges full of convicts. Sleepy and exhausted by their night's labour, the prisoners were limp and sullen, completely silent. Their faces were covered with dew. I now recall several Caucasians with sharp features, wearing fur hats pulled down to their eyebrows.

'Permit me to introduce myself,' said an official. 'I am the college registrar D.'

He was my first Sakhalin acquaintance, a poet, author of a denunciatory poem entitled 'Sakhalinó,' which begins: 'Tell me, Doctor, was it not in vain . . .' Later he often visited me and accompanied me around Alexandrovsk and nearby places, relating anecdotes and endlessly reading his own compositions. During the long winter nights he writes progressive stories. On occasion he enjoys informing people that he is the college registrar and is in charge of the tenth grade. When a woman who had visited him on business called him Mr D., he was insulted and angrily screamed, 'I'm not Mr D. to you, but "your worship."' While strolling along the shore I questioned him about life on Sakhalin, about what was happening, but he only sighed ominously and said, 'You will see!'

The sun was high. Yesterday's fog and darkness, which had so terrified me, vanished in the brilliance of the early morning. The dense, clumsy Zhonkiyer with its lighthouse, 'The Three Brothers' and the high, craggy shores which were visible for tens of versts on both sides, the transparent mist on the mountains and the smoke from the fires did not present such a horrifying scene in the bright sunlight.

There is no harbour here, and the coast is dangerous. This fact was impressively demonstrated by the presence of the Swedish ship *Atlas*, which was wrecked shortly before my arrival and now lay broken on the shore. Boats usually anchor a verst from shore and rarely any nearer. There is a pier, but it is only usable by cutters and barges. It is a large pier, several sazhens long, and T-shaped. Thick log piles had been securely driven into the sea bottom, in the form of squares, which were filled with stone. The top was covered with planking, and there were freight-car rails running the length of the pier. A charming building, the pier office, sits on the wide end of the T; here also stands a tall black mast. The construction is solid, but not permanent. I was told that during a heavy storm the waves sometimes reach the windows of the building and the spray even reaches the yardarm of the mast; the entire pier trembles.

Along the shore near the pier some 50 convicts were wandering, obviously idle; some were in overalls, others in jackets or grey cloth coats. When I approached, they all removed their caps. It is possible that no writer has ever previously received such an honour. Somebody's horse was standing on shore harnessed to a springless carriage. The convicts loaded my luggage in the carriage; a black-bearded man in a coat with his shirt tail hanging got up on the box. We took off.

'Where do you wish to go, your worship?' he asked, turning around and removing his cap.

I asked him if it would be possible to rent lodgings here, even if it was only one room.

'Certainly, your worship, rooms can be rented.'

For the two versts from the pier to the Alexandrovsk Post I travelled along an excellent highway. In comparison to the Siberian roads this is a clean, smooth road with gutters and street lights; it is absolutely luxurious. Adjacent to it runs a railway. However, the scenery along the way is depressing in its barrenness. Along the tops of the mountains and hills encircling the Alexandrovsk valley, through which the River Duyka flows, charred stumps and trunks of larch trees, dried out by fire and wind, project like porcupine quills, while in the valley below there are hillocks covered with sorrel – the remains of swamps which until recently were impassable. The fresh slashes in the earth made by the gutters reveal the complete barrenness of the swampy scorched earth with its half-*vershok* layer of poor soil. There are no spruce trees, no oaks, no maples – only larches, gaunt, pitiful, fretted in precise shapes, and they do not beautify the forests and park-lands as they do in Russia, but serve only to emphasize the poor marshy soil and the severe climate.

The Alexandrovsk Post, or Alexandrovsk for short, is a small, pretty Siberian-type town with 3,000 inhabitants. It does not contain even one stone building. Everything is built of wood, chiefly of larch – the church, the houses and the sidewalks. Here is located the residence of the island's commandant, the centre of Sakhalin civilization. The prison is situated near the main street. Its exterior is quite similar to an army barracks, and as a result Alexandrovsk is completely free of the dismal prison atmosphere which I had expected.

The driver took me to the Alexandrovsk residential district in the suburbs, to the home of one of the peasant exiles. Here I was shown my lodgings. There was a small yard, paved Siberian fashion with timbers and surrounded with awnings. The house contained five spacious, clean rooms and a kitchen, but not a stick of furniture. The landlady, a young peasant woman, brought out a table, and a chair came about five minutes later. 'With firewood the price is 25 roubles; without firewood, 15,' she said.

About an hour later, she brought a samovar and said with a sigh:

'So you have come to visit this godforsaken hole!'

She had come as a little child with her mother, following her father, a convict who has not yet served out his sentence. Now she is married to one of the exiled peasants, a gloomy old man whom I glimpsed crossing the yard. He had some sort of sickness and spent his time lying under the awning and groaning.

'At home in Tambovsk *guberniya* they are probably reaping,' she said. 'Here there is nothing to look at.'

And truly there is nothing interesting to look at. Through the window you could see rows of cabbage plants, and some ugly ditches nearby, and beyond these a gaunt larch tree withering away.

Groaning and holding his side, the landlord entered and began complaining of crop failure, the cold climate, the poor soil. He had completed his prison term and exile, and now owned two houses, some horses and a cow. He employed many workmen and did nothing himself. He had married a young woman and, most important, he had long since been granted permission to return to the mainland – but still he complained.

[...]

The prisoners and the exiles, with some exceptions, walk the streets freely, without chains and without guards; you meet them in groups and singly every step of the way. They are everywhere, in the streets and in the houses. They serve as drivers, watchmen, chefs, cooks and nursemaids. I was not accustomed to seeing so many convicts, and at first their proximity was disturbing and perplexing. You walk past a construction site and you see convicts with axes, saws and hammers. 'Well,' you think, 'they are going to haul me off and murder me!' Or else you are visiting an acquaintance and, not finding him at home, you sit down to write a note, while his convict servant stands waiting behind you, holding the knife with which he has been peeling potatoes in the kitchen. Or it may happen that at about four o'clock in the morning you will wake up and hear a rustling sound, and you look and see a convict approaching the bed on tiptoe, scarcely breathing.

'What's the matter? What do you want?'

'To clean your shoes, your worship.'

Soon I became accustomed to this. Everyone becomes accustomed to it, even women and children. The local ladies think nothing of permitting their children to go out and play in the care of nursemaids sentenced to exile for life.

One correspondent writes that at first he was terrified of every bush, and groped for the revolver under his coat at every encounter with a prisoner on the roads and pathways. Later he calmed down, having come to the conclusion that 'the prisoners are generally nothing more than a herd of sheep, cowardly, lazy, half-starved and servile.' To believe that Russian prisoners do not murder and rob a passerby merely out of cowardice and laziness, one must be either a very poor judge of men or not know them at all.

[. . .]

The days were beautiful with a bright sky and clear air, reminiscent of fall in Russia. The evenings were magnificent. I remember the glowing western sky, the dark-blue sea and a completely white moon rising over the mountains. On such evenings I enjoyed driving along the valley between the post and the village of Novo-Mikhaylovka; the road is smooth, straight; alongside is a railway and a telegraph line. The further we drove from Alexandrovsk, the more the valley narrowed, the shadows deepened; there were giant burdocks in tropical luxuriance; dark mountains rose on all sides. In the distance we could see the flames from coke fires, and there were more flames from a forest fire. The moon rose. Suddenly a fantastic scene. Coming toward us along the railway was a convict, riding in a small cart, dressed in white and leaning on a pole. He stopped abruptly.

'Isn't it time to turn back?' asked my convict driver.

Then he turned the horses, and glancing up at the mountains and the fires, he said:

'It is lonesome here, your worship. It is much better at home in Russia.'

ii. The Prison Settlements of Northern Sakhalin

The second district of Northern Sakhalin is located on the other side of a ridge of the mountain range and is called Tymovsk, because its settlements lie along the Tym River, which falls into the Okhotsk Sea. As you drive from Alexandrovsk to Novo-Mikhaylovka, the mountain ridge rises before you and blocks out the horizon, and what you see from there is called the Pilinga. From the top of the Pilinga a magnificent panorama opens out with the Duyka valley and the sea on one side, and on the other a vast plain which is watered by the Tym and its tributaries for more than 200 versts. This plain is far more interesting than Alexandrovsk. The water, the many kinds of timber forests, the grasses which grow higher than a man, the fabulous abundance of fish and coal deposits suggest the possibility of a satisfying and pleasant life for a million people. That is the way it should be, but the frozen currents of the Okhotsk Sea and the ice floes floating on the eastern shore even in June attest with incontrovertible clarity to the fact that when nature created Sakhalin man and his welfare was the last thing in her mind. If it were not for the mountains, the plain would be a tundra, colder and bleaker than around Viakhty.

The first person to visit the Tym River and describe it was Lieutenant Boshnyak. In 1852 he was sent here by Nevelskoy to verify information obtained from Gilyaks about coal deposits and to cross the island all the way to the shore of the Okhotsk Sea, where there was said to be a beautiful harbour. He was given a dog team, hardtack for thirty-five days, tea and sugar, a small hand compass and a cross. With these came Nevelskoy's parting words of encouragement: 'As long as you have hardtack to quieten your hunger and a mug of water to drink, then with God's help you will find it possible to do your job.'

Having made his way down the Tym to the eastern shore and back, he somehow reached the western shore, completely worn out and famished, and with abscesses on his legs. The starving dogs refused to go any farther. He spent Easter day huddled in the corner of a Gilyak yurt, utterly exhausted. His hardtack was gone, he could not communicate with the Gilyaks, his legs were giving him agonies of pain. What was most interesting about Boshnyak's explorations was, quite obviously, the explorer himself, his youth – he was only twenty-one years old – and his supremely heroic devotion to his task. At the time the Tym was covered with deep snow, for it was March . . .

[. . .]

In 1881 the zoologist Polyakov carried out some serious and extensive explorations of the Tym from a scientific and practical point of view. He left Alexandrovsk on July 24, driving oxen, and crossed the Pilinga with the greatest difficulty. There were only footpaths, and these were climbed by convicts carrying provisions on their backs from the Alexandrovsk district to the Tymovsk.

The elevation of the ridge is 2,000 feet. On a Tym tributary, the Admvo, close to the Pilinga, stood the Vedernikovsky way station, of which only one position has survived, the office of the station guard.

The Tym tributaries are fast flowing, tortuous and full of rapids. It is impossible to use boats. Therefore it was necessary for Polyakov to go by oxen to the Tym River. From Derbinskoye he and his companion used a boat throughout the whole length of the river.

It is tiresome to read his account of this journey because of the exactitude with which he recorded all the rapids and sandbanks. In the 272 versts from Derbinskoye to the sea he was forced to overcome 110 obstacles: 11 rapids, 89 sandbanks and 10 places where the water was dammed by drifting trees and bushes. This means that on the average of every two miles the river is either shallow or choked up. Near Derbinskoye it is 20–25 sazhens wide: the wider the river, the shallower. The frequent bends and turns, the rapid flow and the shallows offer no hope that it will ever be navigable in the real sense of the word. In Polyakov's opinion it would probably be used only for floating rafts. Only the last 70 to 100 versts from the mouth of the river, where it is least favourable for colonization, are deeper and straighter. Here the flow is slower, and there are no rapids or sandbanks. A steam cutter or even a shallow-draft tugboat could use this part of the river.

When the rich fisheries in the neighbourhood fall into the hands of capitalists, serious attempts will probably be made to clear and deepen the waterway. Perhaps a railroad will be built along the river to its mouth, and there is no doubt that the river will repay all these expenditures with interest. But this is far in the future. Under existing conditions, when we consider only the immediate future, the riches of the Tym are almost an illusion. It offers disappointingly little to the penal colony. The Tymovsk settler lives under the same starvation conditions as the Alexandrovsk settler.

According to Polyakov, the Tym River valley is dotted with lakes, bogs, ravines and pits. It has no straight and level expanses overgrown with nutritious fodder grasses, it has no fertile meadows watered by spring floods, and only rarely are sedge-covered meadows found – these are islands overgrown with coarse grass. A thick coniferous forest covers the slopes of the hill. On these slopes we find birches, willows, elms, aspens and entire stands of poplars. The poplars are extremely tall. They are undermined at the banks and fall into the water, where they look like bushes and beaver dams. The bushes here are the bird cherry, the osier, the sweetbrier, the hawthorn ... Swarms of mosquitoes are everywhere. There was frost on the morning of August 1.

The closer you get to the sea, the sparser the vegetation. Slowly the poplar vanishes, the willow tree becomes a bush; the general scene is dominated by the sandy or turfy shore with whortleberries, cloudberries and moss. Gradually the river widens to 75–100 sazhens; now the tundra has taken over, the coastline consists of lowlands and marshes ... A freezing wind blows in from the ocean.

The Tym falls into Nyisky Bay, or the Tro, a small watery wasteland which is the doorway to the Okhotsk Sea, or, which is the same thing, into the Pacific Ocean. The first night Polyakov spent on the shores of the bay was bright and chilly, and a small twin-tailed comet glistened in the sky. Polyakov does not describe the thoughts which crowded in upon him as he enjoyed the sight of the comet and listened to the sounds of the night. Sleep overtook him. On the next day fate rewarded him with an unexpected spectacle. At the mouth of the bay stood a dark ship with some white strakes; the rigging and deckhouse were beautiful; a tied live eagle sat on the prow.

The shore of the bay made a dismal impression on Polyakov. He calls it a typically characteristic example of a polar landscape. The vegetation is meagre and malformed. The bay is separated from the sea by a long, narrow sandy tongue of land created by dunes, and beyond this slip of land the morose, angry sea has spread itself boundlessly for thousands of versts. When a little boy has been reading Mayne Reid and his blanket falls off during the night, he starts shivering, and it is then that he dreams of such a sea. It is a nightmare! The surface is leaden, over it there hangs a monotonous grey sky, and the savage waves batter the wild treeless shore. The waves roar, and once in a great while the black shape of a whale or a seal flashes through them.

Today there is no need to cross the Pilinga by climbing over steep hills and through gulleys in order to reach the Tymovsk district. I have already stated that people nowadays travel from Alexandrovsk to the Tymovsk district through the Arkovo valley and change horses at the Arkovo way station. The roads here are excellent and the horses can travel swiftly.

The first settlement of the Tymovsk region lies sixteen miles past the Arkovo way station bearing the Oriental fairy-tale name of Upper Armudan. It was founded in 1884 and consists of two parts which have spread along the slopes of the mountain near the Armudan River, a tributary of the Tym. It has 178 inhabitants: 123 male and 55 female. There are 78 homesteads with 28 co-owners. Settler Vasilyev even has two co-owners. In comparison with Alexandrovsk, the majority of the Tymovsk settlements, as the reader will see, have many co-owners or half-owners, few women and very few legally married families. In Upper Armudan, of 48 families, only 9 are legal. There are only three free women who followed their husbands, and it is the same in Krasny Yar or Butakovo, which are no more than a year old. This insufficiency of women and families in the Tymovsk settlements is often astounding, and does not conform with the average number of women and families on Sakhalin. It cannot be explained by any local or economic conditions, but by the fact that newly arrived prison parties are sorted out in Alexandrovsk, and the local authorities, according to the proverb that 'your own shirt is nearest to your body,' retain the majority of the women in their own district and 'keep the best for themselves; the worst they send to us,' as a Tymovsk official told me.

The huts in Upper Armudan are either thatched or

covered with tree bark; some windows have no panes or are completely boarded up. The poverty is terrible. Twenty of the men do not live at home. They have gone elsewhere to earn a livelihood. Only 60 desyatins of land have been cultivated for all 75 homesteads and 28 co-owners; 183 poods of grain have been sown, which is less than 2 poods per household. It is beyond my understanding how grain can be grown here, however much is sown. The settlement is high above sea level and is not protected from northern winds; the snow melts two weeks later than in the neighbouring settlement of Malo-Tymovo. In order to fish, they travel 20 to 25 versts to the Tym River in the summer. They hunt fur animals more for sport than for gain, and so little accrues to the economy of the settlement that it is scarcely worth talking about.

I found the householders and the members of their households at home; none of them were occupied even though it was not a holiday, and it seemed that during the warm August weather all of them, from the youngest to the oldest, could have found work either in the field or on the Tym, where the periodic fish were running. The householders and their cohabitants were obviously bored and eager to sit down and discuss anything at all. They laughed from boredom and sometimes cried. They are failures, and most of them are neurasthenics and whiners, 'alienated persons.' Forced idleness has slowly become a habit and they spend their time waiting for good sea weather, become fatigued, have no desire to sleep, do nothing, and are probably no longer capable of doing anything except shuffling cards. It is not strange that card-playing flourishes in Upper Armudan and the local players are famous all over Sakhalin. Because of lack of money they play for small stakes, but make up for this by playing continually, as in the play *Thirty Years, or the Life of a Card Player*. I had a conversation with one of the most impassioned and indefatigable card-players, a settler called Sizov:

'Your worship, why don't they send us to the mainland?' he asked.

'Why do you want to go there?' I asked jokingly. 'You'll have no one to play cards with.'

'That's where the real games are.'

'Do you play faro?' I asked, and held my tongue.

'That's right, your worship, I play faro.'

Later, upon leaving Upper Armudan, I asked my convict driver:

'Do they play for winnings?'

'Naturally, for winnings.'

'But what do they lose?'

'What do you mean? Why, they lose their government rations, their smoked fish! They lose their food and clothing and sit about in hunger and cold.'

'And what do they eat?'

'Why, sir, when they win, they eat; when they lose, they go to sleep hungry.'

Along the lower reaches of the same tributary there is a smaller settlement, Lower Armudan. I arrived late at night and slept in a garret in the jail because the jailer did not permit me to stay in a room. 'It's impossible to sleep here, your worship; the bugs and cockroaches win all the time!' he said helplessly, spreading his hands wide. 'Please go up to the tower.' I climbed to the tower on a ladder, which was soaked and slippery from the rain. When I descended to get some tobacco I saw the 'winning creatures,' and such things are perhaps only possible on Sakhalin. It seemed as though the walls and ceiling were covered with black crêpe, which stirred as if blown by a wind. From the rapid and disorderly movements of portions of the crêpe you could guess the composition of this boiling, seething mass. You could hear rustling and a loud whispering, as if the insects were hurrying off somewhere and carrying on a conversation.

There are 101 settlers in Lower Armudan: 76 male and 25 female. There are 47 homesteaders with 23 co-owners. Four families are married; 15 live as cohabitants. There are only two free women. There are no inhabitants between 15 and 20 years of age. The people live in dire poverty. Only six of the houses are covered with planking; the rest are covered with tree bark and, as in Upper Armudan, some have no windowpanes or are boarded up. My records include not a single labourer. Obviously the householders do nothing. In order to find work, 21 of them have left. Since 1884, when the settlement was founded, only 37 desyatins of arable land have been cleared – i.e., one-half desyatin per homestead. One hundred and eighty-three poods of winter grain and summer corn have been sown. The settlement in no way resembles an agricultural village. The local inhabitants are a disorganized rabble of Russians, Poles, Finns and Georgians, starving and ragged, who came together not of their own volition but by chance, after a shipwreck.

The next settlement along the route lies on the Tym. Founded in 1880, it was named Derbinskoye in honour of the jailer Derbin, who was murdered for his cruelty. He was still young, but a brutish, stern and implacable fellow. The people who knew him recall that he always walked around the prison and on the streets with a stick which he used for beating people. He was murdered in the bakery. He defended himself and fell into the fermenting bread batter, bloodying the dough. His death was greeted with great rejoicing by the convicts, who donated a purse of 60 roubles to the murderer.

There is nothing else amusing in Derbinskoye. It lies on a flat and narrow piece of land, once covered with a thick birch and ash forest. Below, there is a wide stretch of marshland, seemingly unfit for settlement, once thickly covered with fir and deciduous trees. They had scarcely finished cutting down the forest and clearing stumps in order to build the huts, the jail and the government storehouse, and draining the area, when they were forced to battle with a disaster which none of the colonizers had foreseen. During the spring, the high water of the Amga stream flooded the entire settlement. They had to dig another bed and re-channel it. Now Derbinskoye has an area of more than a square verst and resembles a real Russian village.

You enter by a splendid wooden bridge; the stream babbles, the banks are green with willows, the streets are wide, the huts have plank roofs and gardens. There are new prison buildings, all kinds of storehouses and warehouses, and the house of the prison warden stands in the middle of the settlement, reminding you not so much of a prison as of a manorial estate. The warden is continually going from warehouse to warehouse, and he clanks his keys exactly like a landlord in the good old days who guards his stores day and night. His wife sits near the house in the front garden, majestic as a queen, and she sees that order is kept. Right in front of her house, in an open hothouse, she can see her fully ripened watermelons. The convict gardener Karatayev tends them with indulgence and with a slavish diligence. She can see the convicts fishing in the river, bringing back healthy, choice salmon called *serebryanka* [silver fish], which are then cured and given to the officials; they are not given to the convicts. Near the garden play little girls dressed like angels. A convict dressmaker, convicted for arson, sews their clothes. There is a feeling of quiet contentment and ease. These people walk softly like cats, and they also express themselves softly, in diminutives: little fish, little cured fish, little prison rations . . .

There are 739 inhabitants in Derbinskoye, 442 male and 297 female. Altogether, including the prison population, there is a total of about 1,000. There are 250 householders and 58 co-owners. In its outward aspects as well as in the age groups of the inhabitants and, generally, in all the statistics concerning the place, it is one of the few settlements on Sakhalin which can seriously be called a settlement and not a haphazard rabble of people. It has 121 legitimate families. Twelve of them are free, and among the legally married, free women predominate. There are 103 free women. Children comprise one-third of the population.

However, in attempting to understand the economic status of the Derbinskoye inhabitants, you have to confront the various chance circumstances, which play their major and minor roles as they do in other Sakhalin settlements. Here natural law and economic laws appear to take second place, ceding their priority to such accidental variables as the greater or lesser number of unemployables, the number of sick people, the number of robbers, the number of former citizens forced to become farmers, the number of old people, their proximity to the prison, the personality of the warden, etc., etc., and all of these conditions can change every five years or even less than five years. Those who completed their sentences prior to 1881 were the first to settle here, carrying on their backs the bitter past of the settlement, and they suffered, and gradually took over the better land and homesteads. Those who arrived from Russia with money and families are able to live well. The 220 desyatins of land and the yearly production of 3,000 poods of fish, as shown in the records, obviously pertain to the economic position of these homesteaders. The remainder of the inhabitants, more than one-half of the population of Derbinskoye, are starving, in rags, and give the impression of being useless and superfluous; they are hardly alive, and they prevent others from living. In our own Russian villages even fires produce no such sharp distinctions.

It was raining, cold and muddy when I arrived in Derbinskoye and visited the huts. Because of his own small quarters, the warden gave me lodging in a new, recently completed warehouse, which was stored with Viennese furniture. They gave me a bed and a table, and put a latch on the door so that I could lock myself in from inside.

All evening to two o'clock in the morning I read or copied data from the list of homesteads and the alphabetical list of the inhabitants. The rain fell continually, rattling on the roof, and once in a while a belated prisoner or soldier passed by, slopping through the mud. It was quiet in the warehouse and in my soul, but I had scarcely put out the candle and gone to bed when I heard a rustling, whispering, knocking, splashing sound, and deep sighs. Raindrops fell from the ceiling on to the latticework of the Viennese chairs and made a hollow, ringing sound, and after each such sound someone whispered in despair: 'Oh, my God, my God!' Next to the warehouse was the prison. Were the convicts coming at me through an underground passage? But then there came a gust of wind, the rain rattled even more strongly, somewhere a tree rustled – and again, a deep, despairing sigh: 'Oh, my God, my God!'

In the morning I went out on the steps. The sky was grey and overcast, the rain continued to fall, and it was muddy. The warden walked hurriedly from door to door with his keys.

'I'll give you such a ticket you'll be scratching yourself for a week,' he shouted. 'I'll show you what kind of ticket you'll get!'

These words were intended for a group of twenty

prisoners who, from the few phrases I overheard, were pleading to be sent to the hospital. They were ragged, soaked by the rain, covered with mud and shivering. They wanted to demonstrate in mime exactly what ailed them, but on their pinched, frozen faces it somehow came out false and crooked, although they were probably not lying at all. 'Oh, my God, my God!' someone sighed, and my nightmare seemed to be continuing. The word 'pariah' comes to mind, meaning that a person can fall no lower. During my entire sojourn on Sakhalin only in the settlers' barracks near the mine and here, in Derbinskoye, on that rainy, muddy morning, did I live through moments when I felt that I saw before me the extreme limits of man's degradation, lower than which he cannot go.

In Derbinskoye there is a convict, a former baroness, whom the local women call 'the working baroness.' She lives a simple, labourer's life, and they say she is content with her circumstances. One former Moscow merchant who once had a shop on Tverskaya-Yamskaya told me with a sigh, 'The racing season is on in Moscow,' and then, turning to the settlers, he began to explain what kind of races they were and how many people go on Sundays to the racecourse along Tverskaya-Yamskaya. 'Believe me, your worship,' he said, his excitement mounting as he discussed the racecourse, 'I would give everything, my whole life, if I could see not Russia, not Moscow, but the Tverskaya!'

In Derbinskoye there live two people called Emelyan Samokhvalov, who are related to one another, and I remember that in the yard of one of them I saw a rooster tied up by its legs. The people of Derbinskoye are amused by the fact that these two Emelyan Samokhvalovs were by a strange and very complex combination of events brought together from the opposite ends of Russia to Derbinskoye, bearing the same name and being related to one another.

On August 27, General Kononovich arrived in Derbinskoye with the commandant of the Tymovsk district, A. M. Butakov, and another young official. All three were intelligent and interesting people. The four of us went on a small trip. From beginning to end we were beset with so much discomfort that it turned out to be not a trip at all; it was a parody of an expedition.

First of all, it was pouring. It was muddy and slippery; everything you touched was soaking wet. Water leaked through our collars after running down our necks; our boots were cold and wet. To smoke a cigarette was a complicated, difficult affair which was accomplished only when we all helped one another. Near Derbinskoye we got into a rowboat and went down the Tym. On the way we stopped to inspect the fisheries, a water mill and ploughland belonging to the prison. I will describe the fishing elsewhere; we all agreed the water mill was wonderful; and the fields were nothing special, being interesting only because they were so small; a serious homesteader would regard them as child's play.

The river was swift, and the four rowers and the steersman worked in unison. Because of the speed and frequent bends in the river, the scenery changed every minute. We were floating along a mountain taiga river, but all of its wild charms, the green banks, the steep hills and the lone motionless figures of the fishermen, I would have enthusiastically exchanged for a warm room and dry shoes, especially since the landscape was monotonous, not novel to me, and, furthermore, it was covered with grey, rainy mist. A. M. Butakov sat on the bow with a rifle and shot at wild ducks which were startled at our approach.

Northeast from Derbinskoye along the Tym there are only two settlements to date: Voskresenskoye and Uskovo. To settle the Tym up to its mouth would require at least thirty such settlements with ten versts between each of them. The administration plans to set up one or two every year, connecting them with a road which will eventually span the distance between Derbinskoye and Nyisky Bay. The road will bring life and stand guard over a whole series of settlements. As we came close to Voskresenskoye, a guard stood at attention, obviously expecting us. A. M. Butakov shouted to him that on returning from Uskovo we would spend the night there and that he should prepare more straw.

A little while later, the air was strongly permeated with the stench of rotting fish. We were approaching the Gilyak village of Usk-vo, the former name of the present Uskovo. We were met on shore by Gilyaks, their wives, children and bobtailed dogs, but our coming was not regarded with the same amazement as the coming of the late Polyakov. Even the children and the dogs looked at us calmly.

The Russian colony is two versts from the riverbank. In Uskovo the same conditions exist as in Krasny Yar. The street is wide with many tree trunks still to be uprooted, full of hillocks, covered with forest grass, and on each side stand unfinished huts, felled trees and piles of rubble. All new construction on Sakhalin gives the impression of having been destroyed by an enemy or else of being long since abandoned. Only the fresh, bright colours of the hut frames and the shavings give evidence that something quite opposite to destruction is taking place.

Uskovo has 77 inhabitants, 59 male and 18 female, 33 householders and 20 other persons – in other words, co-owners. Only nine have families. When the people of Uskovo gathered around the jail, where we were taking tea, and when the women and children, being more curious, came up front, the crowd looked like a gypsy camp. Among the women there were actually several dark-skinned gypsies with sly, hypocritically sorrowful faces, and almost all the children were gypsies. Uskovo has a few convict gypsies whose bitter fate is shared by their families, who followed them voluntarily. I was slightly acquainted with two or three of the gypsy women. A week before my arrival at Uskovo I had seen them in Rykovskoye with rucksacks on their backs begging at people's windows.

The Uskovo inhabitants live very poorly. Only eleven desyatins of land are cultivated for grain and kitchen gardens – that is, almost one-fifth of a desyatin per homestead. All live at government expense, receiving prison rations which are not acquired cheaply because they have to carry them on their backs over the roadless taiga from Derbinskoye.

After a rest, we set out at five o'clock in the afternoon on foot for Voskresenskoye. The distance is short, only six versts, but because of my inexperience in walking through the taiga I began to feel tired after the first verst. It was raining heavily. Immediately after leaving Uskovo we had to cross a stream about a sazhen wide on thin, crooked logs. My companions crossed safely, but I slipped and got my boot full of water. Before us lay a long, straight road cut through the forest for a projected highway. There was literally not one sazhen which you could walk without being thrown off balance or stumbling: hillocks, holes full of water, stiff tangles of bushes or roots treacherously concealed under the water, and against these you stumble as against a door-step. The most unpleasant of all were the windfalls and the piles of logs cut down in order to carve out the road. You climb up one pile, sweat, and go on walking through the mud, and then you find another pile of logs and there is no way of bypassing it. So you start climbing again, while your companions shout that you are going the wrong way, it should be either left or right of the pile, etc. At the beginning I tried not to get my other boot full of water, but soon I gave up and resigned myself to it. I could hear the laboured breathing of the three settlers who were following behind, carrying our belongings. I was fatigued by the oppressive weather, shortness of breath and thirst. We walked without our service caps; it was easier.

The breathless general sat down on a thick log. We

sat down beside him. We gave a cigarette to each of the settlers, who dared not sit down.

'Well, it's hard going!'

'How many versts to Voskresenskoye?'

'Three more.'

A. M. Butakov walked the most briskly. He had formerly covered tremendous distances over the taiga and tundra, and a six-verst hike was nothing to him. He described his trip along the Poronay River and around Terpeniya Bay. The first day you are exhausted, all your strength gone, the second day your entire body aches but it is already becoming easier to walk; on the third and following days you feel you have sprouted wings, you are not walking but are being carried along by some unknown force, although your legs continue to get entangled in the merciless marsh grass and stuck in swamps.

Halfway it began to grow dark and soon we were surrounded by pitch darkness. I gave up hope that we would ever end our trip, and just groped ahead, splashing in water to my knees, and bumping into logs. Here and there the will-o'-the-wisps gleamed and flickered; entire pools and tremendous rotting trees were lit with phosphorescent colours and my boots were covered with moving sparks which shimmered like the glow-worms on a midsummer night.

But, thank God, at last a light shone in front of us, and was not phosphorescent, but a real light. Someone shouted at us, and we answered. The warden appeared with a lantern. Across pools brightly lit by his lantern, he came with large strides to lead us across the whole of Voskresenskoye, which was barely visible in the darkness, until at last we reached his quarters.

My companions had brought with them a change of clothing. When they reached the warden's quarters they hastened to change. But I had nothing with me, although I was literally soaked through. We drank some tea, talked a bit and went to sleep. There was only one bed in the warden's quarters, and this was taken by the general, while we ordinary mortals went to sleep on straw heaped on the floor.

Voskresenskoye is twice as large as Uskovo. Inhabitants, 183: 175 male and 8 female. There are 7 free families but not one legally married. There are few children in the settlement and only one little girl. It has 97 homesteaders and 77 co-owners.

iii. The Gilyak Tribe

Both of the northern districts, as the reader may readily see from my survey of the settlements, cover an area equal to a small Russian district. It is impossible to compute the area of both of them because there are no northern and southern boundaries. Between the administrative centres of both districts, the Alexandrovsk Post and Rykovskoye, there is a distance of 60 versts by the shorter route which crosses the Pilinga, while across the Arkovskaya valley it is 74 versts. In this kind of country these are large distances. Without considering Tangi and Vangi, even Palevo is considered a distant settlement. Meanwhile the newly founded settlements to the south of Palevo on the Poronaya tributaries raise the question of whether a new district will have to be established.

As an administrative unit, a Sakhalin district corresponds to a Russian district. According to the Siberian way of thinking, this term can only be applied to a postal distance which cannot be travelled in under a month, as for example the Anadyrsky district. To a Siberian official working alone in an area of 200 to 300 versts, the breaking up of Sakhalin into small districts would be a luxury. The Sakhalin population, however, lives under exceptional conditions and the administrative mechanism is far more complicated than in the Anadyrsky district. The need to break up the penal colonies into small administrative units has been shown by experience, and this has proved, in addition to other matters to be explained later, that the shorter the distances in the penal colony, the easier and more effective is the administration. Also, a breakup into smaller districts has the effect of enlarging the number of officials, and the result is an influx of new people who inevitably have a beneficial influence on the colony. And so with a quantitative increase of intelligent people on the staff, there occurs a significant increase in quality.

When I arrived in Sakhalin I heard a great deal of talk about a newly projected district. They described it as the Land of Canaan, because the plan called for a road which would cross the entire region southward along the Poronaya River. It was believed that the convicts at Dué and Voyevodsk would be transferred to the new district, and these horrifying places would become nothing more than a memory. Also, the mines would be taken away from the 'Sakhalin Company,' which had long since broken its contract, and then the mines would be worked by convicts and settlers as a collective enterprise.

Before completing my report on Northern Sakhalin, I feel I should discuss briefly a people who have lived here at different times and continue to live here outside the penal colony.

In the Duyka valley Polyakov found chipped obsidian knives, stone arrows, grinding stones, stone axes and other objects. He came to the conclusion that a people who did not use metal lived in the Dué valley in ancient times; they belonged to the Stone Age. Shards, the bones of dogs and bears, sinkers from large fishing nets, which were found in these formerly inhabited areas, indicate that they made pottery, hunted bear, went fishing and had hunting dogs. Clearly they derived flint from their neighbours on the mainland and on the neighbouring islands, because flint does not exist on Sakhalin. Probably the dogs played the same role in their migration as they do now: they are used for drawing sleighs. In the Tym valley Polyakov found the remnants of primitive structures and crude weapons. He concluded that in Northern Sakhalin 'it is possible for tribes to survive on a relatively low level of intellectual development; the people who lived here for centuries developed ways to protect themselves from cold, thirst and hunger. In all probability these ancient people lived in relatively small communities and were not a completely settled people.'

When sending Boshnyak to Sakhalin, Nevelskoy asked him to verify the rumour about people who had been left on Sakhalin by Lieutenant Khvostov and who had lived, according to the Gilyaks, on the Tym River.

Boshnyak was successful in discovering traces of these people. In one Tym River settlement the Gilyaks exchanged four pages torn from a prayerbook for three arshins of nankeen cloth, saying the prayerbook had been the property of Russians who had once lived there. On the title page, in barely legible script, were the words: 'We, Ivan, Danilo, Pyotr, Sergey and Vasily, were landed in the Aniva settlement of Tomari-Aniva by Khvostov on August 17, 1805. We moved to the Tym River in 1810 when the Japanese arrived in Tomari.' Later, exploring the area where the Russians had lived,

Boshnyak concluded that they had lived in three huts and cultivated gardens. The natives told him that the last of the Russians, Vasily, died recently, that they were fine people, that they went fishing and hunting with the natives and dressed native fashion except for cutting their hair. Elsewhere the natives informed him that two of the Russians had had children with native women. Today the Russians left by Khvostov on Northern Sakhalin have been forgotten and nothing is known of their children.

Boshnyak adds that as a result of his constant inquiries concerning any Russians settled on the island, he learned from natives in the Tangi settlement that some thirty-five or forty years ago there had been a shipwreck, the crew were saved and they built themselves first a house and later a boat. They made their way across La Pérouse to the Tatar Strait by boat and they were again shipwrecked near the village of Mgachi. This time only one man was saved. His name was Kemets. Not long afterward two Russians came from the Amur. Their names were Vasily and Nikita, and they joined Kemets and built themselves a house in Mgachi. They hunted game professionally and traded with the Manchurians and Japanese.

One Gilyak showed Boshnyak a mirror supposedly given to his father by Kemets. The Gilyak would not sell the mirror at any price, saying that he was keeping it as a precious memento of his father's friend. Vasily and Nikita were terrified of the Tsar, and it is obvious that they had escaped from his prisons. All three died on Sakhalin.

The Japanese Mamia-Rinzo learned in 1808 on Sakhalin that Russian boats often appeared on the western side of the island, and the piracy practised by the Russians eventually forced the natives to expel one group of Russians and to massacre another. Mamia-Rinzo names these Russians as Kamutsi, Simena, Momu and Vasire. 'The last three,' says Shrenk, 'are easily recognizable as the Russian names Semyon, Foma and Vasily. Kamutsi is quite similar to Kemets,' in his opinion.

This short history of eight Sakhalin Robinson Crusoes exhausts all the data concerning the free colonization of Northern Sakhalin. If the extraordinary fate of five of Khvostov's sailors, Kemets and the two refugees from prison resembles an attempt at free colonization, this attempt must be regarded as insignificant and completely unsuccessful. The really important fact is that they all lived on Sakhalin for a long time, and to the end of their lives not one of them engaged in agriculture. They lived by fishing and hunting.

To round out the picture I must mention the local indigenous population – the Gilyaks. They live on the western and eastern banks of Northern Sakhalin and along the rivers, especially the Tym.

The villages are old; their names, mentioned in the writings of old authors, have come down without change. However, their way of life cannot be called completely settled, because a Gilyak feels no ties toward his birthplace or to any particular place. They often leave their yurts to practise their trades, and to wander over Northern Sakhalin with their families and dogs. But as to their wanderings, even when they are forced to take long journeys to the mainland, they remain faithful to the island, and the Sakhalin Gilyak differs in language and customs from the Gilyak living on the mainland no less than the Ukrainian differs from the Muscovite.

In view of this, it seems to me that it would not be very difficult to count the number of Sakhalin Gilyaks without confusing them with those who come for trading purposes from the Tatar shore. There would be no harm in taking a census of them every five to ten years; otherwise the important question of the influence of the penal colony on their numbers will long remain open and will be solved in a quite arbitrary fashion.

According to data gathered by Boshnyak in 1856, there were 3,270 Gilyaks on Sakhalin. Fifteen years later Mitsul found only 1,500, and the latest data which I obtained from the prison copy of *Statistical Records of Foreigners*, 1889, showed there were only 320 Gilyaks in both regions. If these figures hold true, not one Gilyak will remain in ten or fifteen years' time. I cannot judge the correctness of the figures given by Boshnyak and Mitsul, but the official figure of 320 can have no significance whatsoever. There are several reasons for this. Statistics on foreigners are calculated by clerks who have neither the educational background nor the practical knowledge to do it, and they are given no instructions. When they gather information at the Gilyak settlements, they naturally conduct themselves in an overbearing manner. They are rude and disagreeable, in contrast to the polite Gilyaks, who do not permit an arrogant and domineering attitude toward people. Because they are averse to any kind of census or registration, considerable skill is needed in handling them. Also, the data is gathered by the administration without any definite plan, only in passing, and the investigator uses no ethnographic map but works in his own arbitrary fashion. The data on the Alexandrovsk district includes only those Gilyaks who live south of the Vangi settlement, while in the Tymovsky district they counted only those they found near the Rykovskoye settlement. Actually they do not live in this settlement, but pass through it on their way to other places.

Undoubtedly the number of Sakhalin Gilyaks is constantly decreasing, and this judgment can be made simply by eye-count. How large is this decrease? Why is it taking place? Is it because Gilyaks are becoming extinct, or because they are moving to the mainland or farther north on the island? Due to the lack of actual statistics (and our figures on the destructive influence of Russian colonization can be based only on analogies) it is quite possible that up to the present day Russian influence has been insignificant, almost zero, since the Sakhalin Gilyaks live by preference along the Tym and the eastern shores of the island, which the Russian settlements have not yet reached.

The Gilyaks are neither Mongols nor Tungus, but belong to some unknown race which may once have been powerful and ruled all of Asia. Now, living out their last centuries on a small patch of land, they are only a small remnant. Yet they are a wonderful and cheerful people. Because of their unusual sociability and mobility, the Gilyaks long ago succeeded in having relations with all the neighbouring peoples, and so it is almost impossible to find a pure-blooded Gilyak without Mongol, Tungus or Ainu elements.

A Gilyak's face is round, flat, moonlike, of yellowish cast, with prominent cheekbones, dirty, with slanting eyes and a barely visible beard. His hair is smooth, black, wiry, gathered into a braid at the nape of the neck. His facial expression is not savage; it is always intelligent, gentle, naïvely attentive; he is either blissfully smiling or thoughtfully mournful, like a widow. When he stands in profile with his sparse beard and braid, with a soft, womanish expression, he could be a model for a picture of Kuteykin, and it becomes almost understandable why some travellers regard the Gilyaks as belonging to the Caucasian race.

Anyone who wants to become thoroughly acquainted with the Gilyaks should consult an ethnographic specialist, L. I. Shrenk. I will limit myself to discussing some of the characteristics of local natural conditions, which may be useful as direct or indirect guidance for new colonists.

The Gilyak has a strong, stocky build, and he is of medium or short stature. Height would be of no advantage to him in the taiga. His bones are thick and distinguished by the strong development of his limbs from rowing and tramping over the hills. This exercise strengthens the muscles, and they indicate powerful musculature and a perpetual, intense struggle against nature. His body is lean, without fat. There are no stout or corpulent Gilyaks. All his fat is used for the warmth which a man on Sakhalin must generate in his body in order to compensate for the heat loss caused by the low temperature and the excessive humidity. It is understandable that a Gilyak should require a good deal of fat in his diet. He eats fatty seal meat, salmon, sturgeon and whale fat. He also eats rare meat in large quantities in raw, dry and frozen form, and because he eats coarse food his chewing muscles are unusually well-developed and all his teeth are badly worn. His food consists exclusively of meat but on rare occasions, at home or while carousing, they add Manchurian garlic or berries to their menus. According to Nevelskoy, the Gilyaks consider agriculture a grievous transgression; whoever ploughs the land or plants anything will soon die. But they eat the bread which the Russians introduced to them with relish, as a delicacy, and it is not unusual to see a Gilyak in Alexandrovsk or Rykovskoye carrying a loaf of bread under his arm.

The Gilyak's clothing has been adapted to the cold, damp and rapidly changing climate. In the summer he wears a shirt of blue nankeen or daba cloth with trousers of the same material. Over his back, as insurance against changing weather, he wears either a coat or a jacket made of seal or dog fur. He puts on fur boots. In winter he wears fur trousers. All this warm clothing is cut and sewn so as not to impede his deft and quick movements while hunting or while riding with his dogs. Sometimes, in order to be in fashion, he wears convict overalls. Eighty-five years ago Krusenstern saw a Gilyak dressed in a magnificent silk costume 'with many flowers woven into it.' Today you will not find such a peacock on Sakhalin if you search with a lamp.

As to Gilyak yurts, these again answer the demands of a damp and cold climate. There are both summer and winter yurts. The first are built on stilts, the second are dug-outs with timber walls having the form of a truncated pyramid. The wood outside is covered with sod. These yurts are made of cheap material which is always at hand, and when the necessity arises they have no regret at leaving them. They are warm and dry, and are certainly far superior to the damp and cold huts made of bark in which our convicts live when they are working on roads or in the fields. These summer yurts should positively be recommended for gardeners, charcoal makers, fishermen and all convicts and settlers who work outside the prison and not in their homes.

Gilyaks never wash, with the result that even ethnographers find it difficult to ascertain the colour of their skins. They never wash their underclothing, and their furs and boots look exactly as if they had just been stripped off a dead dog. The Gilyaks themselves exude a heavy, sharp odour and the close proximity of their dwellings is indicated by the foul, almost unbearable odour of drying fish and rotting fish wastes. Usually near every yurt there is a drying contrivance which is filled to the top with flattened fish, which from afar, especially in the sunshine, looks like strings of coral. Krusenstern found huge masses of tiny maggots an inch thick on the ground surrounding these fish driers.

In the winter the yurts are full of pungent smoke issuing from the hearth. In addition, the Gilyak men, their wives and even the children smoke tobacco.

Nothing is known of the diseases and mortality of the Gilyaks, but it may be supposed that the unhealthy, unhygienic circumstances are detrimental to their health. This may be the cause of their short stature, bloated faces, the sluggishness and laziness of their movements; and this is perhaps why the Gilyaks always have weak resistance to epidemics. The devastation on Sakhalin caused by smallpox is well known.

Krusenstern found twenty-seven houses on Sakhalin's northernmost point, between the Elizaveta and Maria capes. In 1860, P. P. Glen, a participant in a wonderful Siberian expedition, found only traces of the settlement, while in other parts of the island, he tells us, he found evidence that there was once a considerable population. The Gilyaks told him that during the past ten years – i.e., after 1850 – the population had been radically reduced by smallpox. It is certain that the terrible smallpox epidemics which devastated Kamchatka and the Kurile Islands did not bypass Sakhalin. Naturally this was not due to the virulence of the smallpox itself but to the Gilyaks' poor ability to resist it. If typhus or diphtheria are brought into the penal colony and reach the Gilyak yurts, the same effect will be achieved as by the smallpox. I did not hear of any epidemics on Sakhalin; it seems there were none for the past twenty years with the exception of an epidemic of conjunctivitis, which can be observed even now.

General Kononovich gave permission to the regional

hospitals to accept non-Russian patients at government expense (Order No. 335, 1890). We have no exact observations of Gilyak diseases, but some inferences can be drawn as to the causes of their diseases: dirtiness, excessive use of alcohol, intercourse with Chinese and Japanese, constant closeness to dogs, traumas, etc., etc.

There is no doubt they have frequent illnesses and require medical assistance, and if circumstances permit them to take advantage of the new order granting them admission to the hospitals, the local doctors will have the opportunity of studying them more closely. Medicine cannot arrest their yearly mortality, but perhaps the doctors may discover the circumstances under which our interference with the lives of these people will be least harmful.

The character of the Gilyaks is described in different ways by different authors, but all agree that they are not aggressive, dislike brawls and quarrels, and live peacefully with their neighbours. When strangers appear, they are always suspicious and apprehensive; nevertheless, they greet them courteously, without any protest, and sometimes they will lie, describing Sakhalin in the worst possible light, hoping in this way to discourage strangers from the island. They embraced Krusenstern's companions, and when L. I. Shrenk became ill, the news quickly spread among the Gilyaks and evoked the deepest sympathy.

They lie only when they are trading or when speaking to someone they look upon with suspicion, who is therefore in their eyes dangerous, but before telling a lie they always look at one another – a distinctive childish trait. All other lying and boasting in daily life, outside of trading, is repugnant to them.

The following incident occurred early one evening. Two Gilyaks, one with a beard and the other with a swollen feminine face, lay on the grass in front of a settler's hut. I was passing by. They called out to me and started begging me to enter the hut and bring out their outer clothing, which they had left at the settler's that morning. They themselves did not dare to go in. I told them I had no right to go into someone's hut in the absence of the owner. They grew silent.

'You are a politician?' asked the feminine-looking Gilyak in bad Russian.

'No.'

'That means you are a *pishi-pishi*?' [*pisar* means clerk] he said, seeing some paper in my hands.

'Yes, I write.'

'How much salary do you get?'

I was earning about 300 roubles a month. I told them the figure. You should have seen the disagreeable and even painful expressions which my answer produced. Both Gilyaks suddenly grabbed their stomachs, and throwing themselves on the ground, they began rolling around exactly as though they had severe stomach cramps. Their faces expressed despair.

'How can you talk that way?' they said. 'Why did you say such an awful thing? That's terrible! You shouldn't do that!'

'What did I say that was bad?' I asked.

'Butakov, the regional superintendent, well, he's a big man, gets 200, while you are not even an official –

a clerk – amounts to nothing, and you get 300! You spoke untruth! You shouldn't do that!'

I tried to explain that a regional superintendent remains in one place and therefore only gets 200 roubles. Although I am just a '*pishi-pishi*,' I have come a long way – 10,000 versts away. My expenses are greater than Butakov's and therefore I need more money. This calmed the Gilyaks. They exchanged glances, spoke together in Gilyak, and stopped suffering. Their faces showed that they finally believed me.

'It's true, it's true!' said the bearded Gilyak briskly. 'That's fine. You may leave now!'

'It's true,' nodded the other. 'You may go!'

When a Gilyak accepts an obligation, he fulfills it properly. There has never been a single case of a Gilyak dumping mail along the road or embezzling the property of others. Polyakov, who had dealings with Gilyak boatmen, wrote that they were most punctilious in fulfilling an obligation, and this is characteristic of them today when we find them unloading government freight for the prisons.

They are clever, intelligent, cheerful, brash, and are never shy in the society of strong and rich men. They do not accept authority, and they do not even understand the meaning of 'older' and 'younger.' In *The History of Siberia*, by I. Fisher, we read that the renowned Polyakov visited the Gilyaks, who were then 'under no foreign domination.' They have a word, *dzhanchin*, which denotes 'your excellency,' and they use it equally to a general or to a rich trader who has a great deal of nankeen and tobacco. Seeing Nevelskoy's picture of the Tsar, they said he must be a strong man who distributes much nankeen and tobacco.

The commandant of the island possesses vast and terrifying powers. Nevertheless, when I was riding with him from Verkhny Armudan to Arkovo, a Gilyak had no compunction about shouting at us imperiously: 'Stop!' Then he asked if we had seen his white dog along the road.

As it is often said and written, Gilyaks have no respect for family seniority. A father does not believe he is senior to his son, and a son does not respect his father, but lives as he pleases. An old mother has no more authority in the yurt than a teenage daughter. Boshnyak wrote that he often saw a son beat his mother and chase her out of the house and no one dared say a word against him. The male members of a family are equal to one another. If you treat Gilyaks to vodka, it must also be served to the very youngest males.

The females are equally without rights, whether it is a grandmother, mother or breast-fed baby girl. They are treated as domestic animals, as chattels, which can be thrown out, sold or kicked like a dog. The Gilyaks pet their dogs, but women – never. Marriage is considered nonsense – much less important, for example, than a drinking bout. It is not accompanied by any religious or superstitious rites. A Gilyak exchanges a spear, a boat or a dog for a young girl, drives her to his yurt and lies down with her on a bearskin – and that is all there is to it. Polygamy is permitted but is not widespread, although there are obviously more women than men. Contempt for women as for a lower creature or possession has come to such a pass that the Gilyak does not consider slavery, in the exact and coarse meaning of the word, as reprehensible. As Shrenk witnessed, the Gilyaks often bring Ainu women home with them as slaves. Plainly a woman is an object of barter, like tobacco or daba cloth. Strindberg, that famous misogynist, who thought women should be slaves of men's desires, follows the Gilyak pattern. If he happened to visit Northern Sakhalin, they would embrace him warmly.

General Kononovich told me he wants to Russify the Sakhalin Gilyaks. I don't know why this is necessary. Furthermore, Russification had already begun long before the general's arrival. It began when some prison wardens, receiving very small salaries, began acquiring expensive fox and sable cloaks at the same time that Russian water jars appeared in Gilyak yurts.

As time passed, the Gilyaks were hired to help in tracking down prisoners who escaped from the prison. There was a reward for capturing them, dead or alive. General Kononovich ordered Gilyaks to be hired as jailers. One of his orders says this is being done because of the dire need for people who are well acquainted with the countryside, and to ease relations between the local authorities and the non-Russians. He told me personally that his new ruling is also aimed at their Russification.

The first ones approved as jailers were the Gilyaks Vaska, Ibalka, Orkun and Pavlinka (Order No. 308, 1889). Later, Ibalka and Orkun were discharged 'for continuous failure to appear at the administrative office

to receive their orders,' and they then approved Sof-
ronka (Order No. 426, 1889). I saw these jailers; they
wore tin badges and revolvers. The most popular and
the one who is seen most often is the Gilyak Vaska, a
shrewd, sly drunkard. One day I went to the shop
supported by the colonization fund and met a large
group of the intelligentsia. Someone, pointing at a shelf
full of bottles, said that if you drank them all down you
would really get drunk, and Vaska smirked fawningly,
glowing with the wild joy of a tippler. Just before my
arrival a Gilyak jailer on duty killed a convict and the
local sages were concerned with only one question:
whether he was shot in the chest or in the back – that
is, whether to arrest the Gilyak or not.

That their proximity to the prison will not Russify
but eventually alienate the Gilyaks does not have to be
proved. They are far from understanding our require-
ments, and there is scarcely any opportunity to explain
to them that convicts are caught, deprived of their
freedom, wounded and killed not because of caprice,
but in the interests of justice. They regard this as
coercion, a display of bestiality, and probably consider
themselves as hired killers.

If it is absolutely necessary to Russify them and if it
cannot be avoided, I believe that when we choose our
methods, our primary concern should not be our own
needs, but theirs. The order permitting them to
become patients in our hospitals, the distribution of
aid in the form of flour and groats, as was done in 1886
when the Gilyaks were starving, and the order not to
confiscate their property for debt, and the remission

of their debts (Order No. 204, 1890), and all similar measures will probably achieve this aim more quickly than tin badges and revolvers.

In addition to the Gilyaks, there are a small number of Oroki, or Orochi, of the Tungus tribe living in Northern Sakhalin. Since they are barely heard of in the colony and since no Russian settlements exist in this area, I merely mention them here.

iv. *The Morality of Sakhalin*

Some convicts bear their punishment with fortitude, readily admit their guilt, and when you ask them why they came to Sakhalin, they usually answer, 'They do not send anyone here for their good deeds.' Others astonish you with their cowardice and the melancholy face they show to the world. They grumble, they weep, are driven to despair, and swear they are innocent. One considers his punishment a blessing because, he says, only in penal servitude did he find God. Another attempts to escape at the first opportunity, and when they catch up with him, he turns on his captors and clubs them. Accidental transgressors, 'unfortunates,' and those innocently sentenced live under one roof with inveterate and incorrigible criminals and outcasts.

When the general question of morality is discussed, we must admit that the exile population produces an extremely mixed and confusing impression, and with the existing means of research it is scarcely possible to form any serious generalizations. The morality of a population is usually judged by statistics of crimes, but even this normal and simple method is useless in a penal colony. The strictly nominal infractions of the law, the self-imposed rules and the transgressions of the convict population living under abnormal and exceptional conditions – all these things which we consider petty violations are regarded as serious crimes in Sakhalin, and conversely a large number of serious crimes committed here are not regarded as crimes at all, because they are considered perfectly normal and inevitable phenomena in the atmosphere of the prison.

The vices and perversions which may be observed among the exiles are those which are peculiar to enslaved, subjected, hungry and frightened people. Lying, cunning, cowardice, meanness, informing, robbery, every kind of secret vice – such is the arsenal which these slavelike people, or at least the majority of them, employ against the officials and guards they despise, fear and regard as their enemies. The exile resorts to deceit in order to evade hard labour or corporal punishment and to secure a piece of bread, a pinch of tea, salt or tobacco, because experience has proved to him that deceit is the best and most dependable strategy in the struggle for existence. Thievery is common and is regarded as a legitimate business.

The prisoners grab up everything that is not well hidden with the tenacity and avarice of hungry locusts, and they give preference to edibles and clothing. They steal from each other in the prison; they steal from settlers, and at their work, and when loading ships. The virtuosity of their dexterous thieving may be judged by the frequency with which they practice their art. One day they stole a live ram and a whole tub of sour dough from a ship in Dué. The barge had not yet left the ship, but the loot could not be found. On another occasion they robbed the commander of a ship, unscrewing the lamps and the ship's compass. On still another occasion they entered the cabin of a foreign ship and stole the silverware. During the unloading of cargo whole bales and barrels vanish.

A convict takes his recreation secretly and furtively. In order to obtain a glass of vodka, which under ordinary circumstances costs only five kopecks, he must surreptitiously approach a smuggler and if he has no money he must pay in bread or clothing. His sole mental diversion – card-playing – can only be enjoyed at night in the light of candle stubs or in the taiga. All secret amusements, when repeated, slowly develop into passions. The extreme imitativeness among the convicts causes one prisoner to infect another and finally such seeming inanities as contraband vodka and card-playing lead to unbelievable lawlessness. As I have already said, kulaks among the convicts often amass fortunes. This means that alongside convicts who possess 30,000 to 50,000 roubles, you find people who systematically squander their food and clothing.

Card-playing has infected all the prisons like an epidemic. The prisons are large gambling houses, while the settlements and posts are their branches. Gambling is exceptionally widespread. They say that during a chance search the organizers of the local card games were found to be in possession of hundreds and thousands of roubles, and they are in direct communication with the Siberian prisons, notably the prison at Irkutsk, where, so the prisoners say, they play 'real' cards.

There are several gambling houses in Alexandrovsk. There was even a scandal in a gambling house on Second Kirpichnaya Street, which is characteristic of similar haunts. A guard lost everything and shot himself. Playing faro dulls the brain and acts like a narcotic. The convict loses his food and clothing, feels neither hunger nor cold, and suffers no pain when he is beaten. And how strange it is that even when they are loading a ship, and the coal barge is bumping broadside against the ship, and the waves are smashing against it and they are growing green with seasickness, even then they play cards on the barge and casual everyday expressions are mingled with words which arise purely from card-playing: 'Push off!' 'Two on the side!' 'I've got it!'

Furthermore, the subservient status of the woman, her poverty and degradation, are conducive to the development of prostitution. When I asked in Alexandrovsk if there were any prostitutes there, they answered, 'As many as you want.' Because of the tremendous demand, neither old age, nor ugliness, nor even tertiary syphilis is an impediment. Even extreme youth is no hindrance. I met a sixteen-year-old girl on a street in Alexandrovsk, and they say she has been engaged in prostitution since she was nine years old. The girl has a mother, but a family background on Sakhalin does not always save a young girl from disaster. They talk about a gypsy who sells his daughters and even haggles over them. One free woman in Alexandrovsk has an 'establishment,' in which only her own daughters operate. In Alexandrovsk corruption is generally of an urban character. There are 'family baths' run by a Jew, and the names of the professional panderers are known.

According to government data, incorrigible criminals, those who have been resentenced by the district court, comprise 8 per cent of the convicts as of

January 1, 1890. Among the incorrigibles were some who have been sentenced three, four, five and even six times. There are 175 persons who through their incorrigibility have spent twenty to fifty years in penal servitude – i.e., 3 percent of the total. But these are exaggerated figures for incorrigibles, since the majority of them were shown to have been resentenced for attempts to escape. And these figures are inaccurate with regard to attempted escapes, because those who have been caught are not always brought to trial but are most frequently punished in the usual fashion. The extent to which the exile population is delinquent or, in other words, criminally inclined is presently unknown.

True, they do try people here for crimes, but many cases are dismissed because the culprits cannot be found, many are returned for additional information or clarification of jurisdiction, or the trial remains at a standstill because the necessary information has not been received from the various Siberian offices. Finally, after a great deal of red tape, the documents go into the archives upon the death of the accused, or if nothing more is heard of him after his escape. Credence is attached to evidence by young people who have received no education, while the Khabarovsk court tries people from Sakhalin *in absentia*, basing its verdict only on documents.

During 1889, 243 convicts were under juridical investigation or on trial, that is, one defendant for every 25 convicts. There were 69 settlers under investigation and on trial, i.e., one in 55. Only 4 peasants were under investigation, i.e., one in 115. From these ratios it is evident that with the easing of his lot and with the transition of the convict to a status giving him more freedom, the chances of being brought to trial are decreased by half each time. All these figures pertain to persons on trial and under investigation, but do not necessarily represent crimes committed in 1889, because the files dealing with these crimes refer to trials begun many years ago and not yet completed. These figures give the reader some idea of the tremendous number of people on Sakhalin who languish year after year in the courts and under investigation, because their cases have been drawn out over a period of years. The reader can well imagine how destructively this system reacts on the economy and on the spirit of the people.

Investigation is usually entrusted to the prison warden's assistant or to the secretary of the police department. According to the island commandant, 'investigations are begun on insufficient information, they are conducted sluggishly and clumsily, and the prisoners are detained without any reason.' A suspect or an accused person is arrested and put in a cell. When a settler was killed at Goly Mys, four men were suspected and arrested. They were placed in dark cold cells. In a few days three were released, and only one was detained. He was put in chains and orders were issued to give him hot food only every third day. Then, by order of the warden, he was given 100 lashes. A hungry, frightened man, he was kept in a dark cell until he confessed. The free woman Garanina was detained in the prison at the same time on suspicion of having murdered her husband. She was also placed in a dark cell and received hot food every third day. When one official questioned her in my presence, she said that she had been ill for a long time and that for some reason they would not permit a doctor to see her. When the official asked the guard in charge of the cells why they had not troubled to get a doctor for her, he answered, 'I went to the honourable warden, but he only said, "Let her croak."'

This incapacity to differentiate imprisonment before trial from punitive imprisonment (and this in a dark cell of a convict prison), the incapacity to differentiate between free people and convicts amazed me especially because the local district commander is a law-school graduate and the prison warden was at one time a member of the Petersburg Police Department.

I visited the cells a second time early in the morning in the company of the island commandant. Four convicts suspected of murder were released from their cells; they were shivering with cold. Garanina, in stockings and without shoes, was shivering and blinking in the light. The commandant ordered her transferred to a room with good light. I saw a Georgian flitting like a shadow around the entrance to the cells. He has been held for five months in the dark hallway on suspicion of poisoning and is awaiting investigation. The assistant prosecutor does not live on Sakhalin and there is nobody to supervise an investigation. The direction and speed of an investigation are totally dependent on various circumstances which have no reference to the case itself. I read in one report that the murder of a certain Yakovleva was committed 'with the intent of robbery with a preliminary attempt at rape, which is evidenced by the rumpled bedding and fresh scratches and impressions of heel spikes on the backboard of the bed.' Such a consideration predetermines the outcome of the trial; an autopsy is not considered necessary in such cases. In 1888 an escaped convict murdered Private Khromatykh and the autopsy was only conducted in 1889 on the demand of the prosecutor when the investigation had been completed and the case brought to trial.

Article 469 of the *Code* permits the local administration to specify and carry out punishment without any formal police investigation for such crimes and offences by criminals for which punishment is due according to the general criminal laws, not excluding the loss of all personal rights and privileges in imprisonment. Generally the petty cases on Sakhalin are judged by a formal police court which is under the authority of the police department. Notwithstanding the broad scope of this local court, which has jurisdiction over all petty crimes as well as over a multitude of cases which are only nominally regarded as petty, the local community does not enjoy justice and lacks a court of law. Where an official has the right, according to law, to flog and incarcerate people without trial and without investigation and even to send them to hard labour in the mines, the existence of a court of law has merely formal significance.

Punishment for serious crimes is decided by the Primorskaya district court, which settles cases only on documentary evidence without questioning the defendants or witnesses. The decision of a district court is always presented for approval to the island commandant, who, if he disagrees with the verdict, settles the case on his own authority. If the sentence is changed, the fact is reported to the ruling senate. If the administration considers a crime as being more serious than it appears to be on the official record, and if it regards the punishment as insufficient according to the *Code on Convicts*, then it petitions for arraignment of the defendant before a court-martial.

The punishment usually inflicted upon convicts and settlers is distinguished by extraordinary severity. Our *Code on Convicts* is at odds with the spirit of the times and of the laws, and this is especially evident in the sections concerning punishment. Punishments which humiliate the offender, embitter him and contribute to his moral degradation, those punishments which have long since been regarded as intolerable among free men, are still being used here against settlers and convicts. It is as though exiles were less subject to the dangers of becoming bitter and callous, and losing their human dignity. Birch rods, whips, chains, iron balls, punishments which shame the victim and cause pain and torment to his body, are used extensively. Floggings with birch rods and whips are habitual for all kinds of transgressions, whether small or large. It is the indispensable mainstay of all punishment, sometimes supplementing other forms of chastisement, or used alone.

The most frequently used punishment is flogging

with birch rods. As shown in the official report, this punishment was imposed on 282 convicts and settlers in Alexandrovsk in 1889 by orders of the administration: corporal punishment, i.e., with birch rods, was inflicted on 265, while 17 were punished in other ways. The administration used birch rods in 94 out of 100 cases. In fact, the number of criminals suffering corporal punishment is far from being accurately recorded in the reports. The reports of the Tymovsky district for 1889 show that only 57 convicts were beaten with birch rods and only 3 are recorded in Korsakov; although the truth is that they flog several people every day in both districts, and sometimes there are 10 a day in Korsakov.

All sort of transgressions may result in a man's getting 30 to 100 strokes with birch rods: nonperformance of the daily work quota (for example, if the shoemaker did not sew his required three pairs of shoes), drunkenness, vulgarity, insubordination . . . If 20 to 30 men fail to complete their work quota, all 20 to 30 are beaten. One official told me:

The prisoners, especially those in irons, like to present absurd petitions. When I was appointed here, I toured the prison and received 50 petitions. I accepted them, and then announced that those whose petitions do not deserve attention would be punished. Only 2 of the petitions proved to be worthwhile, the remainder were nonsense. I ordered 48 men to be flogged. The next time 25 were flogged, and later fewer and fewer, and now they no longer send me petitions. I cured them of the habit.

In the South, as a result of a convict's denunciation, a search was made of another convict's possessions and a diary was found which was presumed to contain drafts of correspondence carried on with friends at home. They gave him 50 strokes with birch rods and kept him 15 days in a dark cell on bread and water. With the knowledge of the district commander, the inspector in Lyutoga gave corporal punishment to nearly everyone. Here is how the island commandant describes it:

The commander of the Korsakov district informed me about the extremely serious instances of excessive authority used by X., who ordered some settlers to receive corporal punishment far beyond the limits set by the law. This instance, shocking in itself, is even more shocking when the circumstances which provoked the punishment are analysed. There had been a quite commonplace and futile brawl between exiled settlers; and it made no difference to him whether he punished the innocent or the guilty, or pregnant women. [Order No. 258, 1888.]

Usually an offender receives 30 to 100 strokes with birch rods. This depends on who gave the order to punish him, the district commander or the warden. The former has the right to order up to 100, the latter up to 30. One warden always gave 30. Once when he was required to take the place of the district commander, he immediately raised his customary allotment to 100, as though this hundred strokes with birch rods was an indispensable mark of his new authority. He did not change the number until the district commander returned, and then in the same conscientious manner he resumed the old figure of 30. Because of its very frequent application, flogging with birch rods has become debased. It no longer causes abhorrence or fear among many prisoners. They tell me that there are quite a number of prisoners who do not feel any pain when they are being flogged with birch rods.

Lashes are used far less frequently and only after a sentence passed by the district courts. From a report of the director of the medical department it appears that in 1889, 'in order to determine the ability to endure corporal punishment ordered by the courts,' 67 prisoners were examined by the doctors. Of all the punishments exacted on Sakhalin this punitive measure is the most abominable in its cruelty and abhorrent circumstances, and the jurists of European Russia who sentence vagrants and incorrigible criminals to be flogged would have renounced this mode of punishment long ago had it been carried out in their presence. But these floggings are prevented from being a scandalous and outrageously sensational spectacle by Article 478 of the *Code*, which specifies that the sentences of the Russian and Siberian courts must be executed in the place where the prisoner is confined.

I saw how they flog prisoners in Dué. Vagrant Prokhorov, whose real name was Mylnikov, a man thirty-five to forty years of age, escaped from the Voyevodsk prison, and after building a small raft, he took off for the mainland. On shore they noticed him in time, and sent a cutter to intercept him. The investigation of his escape began. They took a look at the official records and then they made a discovery: this Prokhorov was actually Mylnikov, who had been sentenced last year by the Khabarovsk district court to 90 lashes and the ball and chain for murdering a Cossack and his two grandchildren. Owing to an oversight the sentence had not yet been carried out. If Prokhorov had not taken it into his head to escape, they might never have noticed their error and he would have been spared a flogging and being chained to an iron ball. Now, however, the execution of the sentence was inevitable.

On the morning of the appointed day, August 13, the warden, the physician and I leisurely approached the prison office. Prokhorov, whose presence in the office had been ordered the previous evening, was sitting on the porch with a guard. He did not know what awaited him. Seeing us, he got up. He may have understood then what was going to happen, because he blanched.

'Into the office!' the warden ordered.

We entered the office. They led Prokhorov in. The doctor, a young German, ordered him to strip and listened to his heart to ascertain how many lashes the prisoner could endure. He decides this question in a minute and then in a businesslike fashion sits down to write his examination report.

'Oh, the poor fellow!' he says sorrowfully in a thick German accent, dipping the pen into the ink. 'The chains must weigh upon you! Plead with the honourable warden and he will order them removed.'

Prokhorov remains silent. His lips are pale and trembling.

'Your hope is in vain,' the doctor continues. 'You all have vain hopes. Such suspicious people in Russia! Oh, poor fellow, poor fellow!'

The report is ready. They include it with the documents on the investigation of the escape. Then follows utter silence. The clerk writes, the doctor and the warden write. Prokhorov does not yet know exactly why he was brought here. Is it only because he escaped, or because of the escape and the old question as well? The uncertainty depresses him.

'What did you dream of last night?' the warden asks finally.

'I forgot, your worship.'

'Now listen,' says the warden, glancing at the official documents. 'On such and such a date you were sentenced to 90 lashes by the Khabarovsk district court for murdering a Cossack . . . And today is the day you are to get them.'

Then he smacks the prisoner on his forehead with the flat of his hand and admonishes him:

'Why did all this have to happen? It's because your head needs to be smarter than it is. You all try to escape and think you will be better off, but it turns out worse.'

We all enter the 'guardhouse,' which is a grey barracks-type building. The military medical assistant, who stands at the door, says in a wheedling voice as though asking a favour:

'Your worship, please let me see how they punish a prisoner.'

In the middle of the guardroom there is a sloping bench with apertures for binding the hands and feet.

The executioner is a tall, solid man, built like an acrobat. His name is Tolstykh. He wears no coat, and his waistcoat is unbuttoned. He nods at Prokhorov, who silently lies down. Tolstykh, taking his time, silently pulls down the prisoner's trousers to the knees and slowly ties his hands and feet to the bench. The warden looks callously out the window, the doctor strolls around the room. He is carrying a vial of medicinal drops in his hands.

'Would you like a glass of water?' he asks.

'For God's sake, yes, your worship.'

At last Prokhorov is tied up. The executioner picks up the lash with three leather thongs and slowly straightens it.

'Brace yourself!' he says softly, and without any excessive motion, as though measuring himself to the task, he applies the first stroke.

'One-ne,' says the warden in his chanting voice of a cantor.

For a moment Prokhorov is silent and his facial expression does not change, but then a spasm of pain runs along his body, and there follows not a scream but a piercing shriek.

'Two,' shouts the warden.

The executioner stands to one side and strikes in such a way that the lash falls across the body. After every five strokes he goes to the other side and the prisoner is permitted a half-minute rest. Prokhorov's hair is matted to his forehead, his neck is swollen. After the first five or ten strokes his body, covered by scars from previous beatings, turns blue and purple, and his skin bursts at each stroke.

Through the shrieks and cries there can be heard the words: 'Your worship! Your worship! Mercy, your worship!'

And later, after 20 or 30 strokes, he complains like a drunken man or like someone in delirium:

'Poor me, poor me, you are murdering me . . . Why are you punishing me?'

Then follows a peculiar stretching of the neck, the noise of vomiting. Prokhorov says nothing; only shrieks and wheezes. A whole eternity seems to have passed since the beginning of the punishment. The warden cries, 'Forty-two! Forty-three!' It is a long way to 90.

I go outside. The street is quite silent, and it seems to me that the heartrending sounds from the guardhouse can be heard all over Dué. A convict wearing the clothing of a free man passes by and throws a fleeting glance in the direction of the guardhouse, terror written on his face and on his way of walking. I return to the guardhouse, and then go out again, and still the warden keeps counting.

Finally, 90! Prokhorov's hands and feet are quickly released and he is lifted up. The flesh where he was beaten is black and blue with bruises and it is bleeding. His teeth are chattering, his face yellow and damp, and his eyes are wandering. When they give him the medicinal drops in a glass of water, he convulsively bites the glass . . . They soak his head with water and lead him off to the infirmary.

'That was for the murder. He'll get another one for escaping,' I was told as we went home.

'I love to see how they execute punishment!' the military medical assistant exclaims joyfully, extremely pleased with himself because he was satiated with the abominable spectacle. 'I love it! They are such scum, such scoundrels. They should be hanged!'

Not only do the prisoners become hardened and brutalized from corporal punishment, but those who inflict the punishment become hardened, and so do the spectators. Educated people are no exception. At any rate, I observed that officials with university training reacted in exactly the same way as the military medical assistants or those who had completed a course in a military school or an ecclesiastical seminary. Others become so accustomed to birch rods and lashes and so brutalized that in the end they come to enjoy the floggings.

They tell a story about one prison warden who whistled when a flogging was being administered in his presence. Another warden, an old man, spoke to the prisoner with happy malice, saying, 'God be with you! Why are you screaming? It's nothing, nothing at all! Brace yourself! Beat him, beat him! Scourge him!' A third warden ordered the prisoner to be tied to the bench by his neck so that he would choke. He administered five or ten strokes and then went out somewhere for an hour or two. Then he came back and gave him the rest.

The courts-martial are composed of local officers

appointed by the island commandant. The documents on the case and the court's verdict are sent to the Governor-General for confirmation. In the old days prisoners languished in their cells for two and three years while awaiting confirmation of the sentence; now their fate is decided by telegraph. The usual sentence of the courts-martial is death by hanging. Sometimes the Governor-General reduces the sentence to 100 lashes, the ball and chain and detention for those on probation with an indefinite term. If a murderer is sentenced to death, the sentence is very seldom commuted. 'I hang murderers!' the Governor-General told me.

On the day before an execution, during the evening and throughout the entire night, the prisoner is prepared for his last journey by a priest. The preparation consists of confession and conversation. One priest told me:

At the beginning of my priestly career, when I was only twenty-five, I was ordered to prepare two convicts for death at the Voyevodsk prison. They were to be hanged for murdering a settler for 1 rouble 40 kopecks. I went into their cell. The task was a new one for me, and I was frightened. I asked the sentry not to close the door and to stand outside. They said, 'Don't be afraid, little father. We won't kill you. Sit down.'

I asked where I should sit and they pointed to the plank bed. I sat down on a water barrel and then gaining courage, I sat on the plank bed between the two criminals. I asked what *guberniya* they came from and other questions, and then I began to prepare them for death. While they were confessing I looked up and saw the men carrying the beams and all the other necessities for the gallows. They were passing just below the window.

'What is that?' the prisoners asked.

'They're probably building something for the warden,' I said.

'No, little father, they're going to hang us. What do you say, little father, do you think we could have some vodka?'

'I don't know,' I said. 'I'll go and ask.'

I went to Colonel L. and told him the prisoners wanted a drink. The colonel gave me a bottle, and so that no one should know about it, he ordered the turnkey to remove the sentry. I obtained a whisky glass from a guard and returned to the cell. I poured out a glass of vodka.

'No, little father,' they said. 'You drink first, or we won't have any.'

I had to drink a jigger, but there was no snack to go with it.

'Well,' they said, 'the vodka brightened our thoughts.'

After this I continued their preparation. I spoke with them an hour, and then another. Suddenly there was the command: 'Bring them out!'

After they were hanged, I was afraid to enter a dark room for a long time.

The fear of death and the conditions under which executions are carried out have an oppressive effect on those sentenced to death. On Sakhalin there has not been a single case where the condemned man went to his death courageously. When the convict Chernosheya, the murderer of the shopkeeper Nikitin, was being taken from Alexandrovsk to Dué before execution, he suffered bladder spasms. He would suffer a spasm and have to stop. One of the accessories in the crime, Kinzhalov, went mad. Before the execution they were clothed in a shroud and the death sentence was read out. One of the condemned men fainted when the death sentence was being read out. After Pazhukin, the youngest murderer, had been dressed in his shroud and the death sentence was read out, it was announced that his sentence had been commuted. How much this man lived through during that brief space of time! The long conversation with the priests at night, the ceremony of confession, the half-jigger of vodka at dawn, the words 'Bring them out,' and then the shroud, and then listening to the death sentence, and all this followed by the joy of commutation. Immediately after his friends were executed, he received 100 lashes, and after the fifth stroke he fell in a dead faint, and then he was chained to an iron ball.

Eleven men were sentenced to death for the murder of some Ainus in the Korsakov district. None of the officers and officials slept on the night before the execution; they visited each other and drank tea. There was a general feeling of exhaustion; nobody found a comfortable place to rest in. Two of the condemned men poisoned themselves with wolfsbane – a tremendous embarrassment to the military officials responsible for the execution of the sentences. The district commander heard a tumult during the night and was then informed that the two prisoners had poisoned themselves. When everyone had gathered around the scaffold just before the execution, the district commander found himself saying to the officer in charge:

'Eleven were sentenced to death, but I see only nine here. Where are the other two?'

Instead of replying in the same official manner, the officer in charge said in a low, nervous voice:

'Why don't you hang me! Hang me . . .'

It was an early October morning, grey, cold and dark. The faces of the prisoners were yellow with fear and their hair was waving lightly. An official read out the death sentence, trembling with nervousness and stuttering because he could not see well. The priest, dressed in black vestments, presented the Cross for all nine to kiss, and then turned to the district commander, whispering:

'For God's sake, let me go, I can't . . .'

The procedure is a long one. Each man must be dressed in a shroud and led to the scaffold. When they finally hanged the nine men, there was 'an entire bouquet' hanging in the air – these were the words of the district commander as he described the execution to me. When the bodies were lifted down the doctors found that one was still alive.

This incident had a peculiar significance. Everyone in the prison, all those who knew the innermost secrets of the crimes committed by the inmates, the hangman and his assistants – all of them knew he was alive because he was innocent of the crime for which he was being hanged.

'They hanged him a second time,' the district commander concluded his story. 'Later I could not sleep
for a whole month.'

THE STORY OF PENGUIN CLASSICS

Before 1946 ...'Classics' are mainly the domain of academics and students, without readable editions for everyone else. This all changes when a little-known classicist, E. V. Rieu, presents Penguin founder Allen Lane with the translation of Homer's *Odyssey* that he has been working on and reading to his wife Nelly in his spare time.

1946 *The Odyssey* becomes the first Penguin Classic published, and promptly sells three million copies. Suddenly, classic books are no longer for the privileged few.

1950s Rieu, now series editor, turns to professional writers for the best modern, readable translations, including Dorothy L. Sayers's *Inferno* and Robert Graves's *The Twelve Caesars*, which revives the salacious original.

1960s The Classics are given the distinctive black jackets that have remained a constant throughout the series's various looks. Rieu retires in 1964, hailing the Penguin Classics list as 'the greatest educative force of the 20th century'.

1970s A new generation of translators arrives to swell the Penguin Classics ranks, and the list grows to encompass more philosophy, religion, science, history and politics.

1980s The Penguin American Library joins the Classics stable, with titles such as *The Last of the Mohicans* safeguarded. Penguin Classics now offers the most comprehensive library of world literature available.

1990s The launch of Penguin Audiobooks brings the classics to a listening audience for the first time, and in 1999 the launch of the Penguin Classics website takes them online to a larger global readership than ever before.

The 21st Century Penguin Classics are rejacketed for the first time in nearly twenty years. This world famous series now consists of more than 1300 titles, making the widest range of the best books ever written available to millions – and constantly redefining the meaning of what makes a 'classic'.

The Odyssey continues ...

The best books ever written

PENGUIN 🐧 CLASSICS

SINCE 1946